CO-DETERMINATION
IN
BUSINESS

Robert J. Kühne

CO-DETERMINATION IN BUSINESS

Workers' Representatives in the Boardroom

PRAEGER

PRAEGER SPECIAL STUDIES • PRAEGER SCIENTIFIC

Library of Congress Cataloging in Publication Data

Kühne, Robert J
    Co-determination in business.

    Bibliography: p.
    Includes index.
    1. Employees' representation in management--Europe.
2. Works councils--Europe. 3. Corporations, American--
Europe--Management. I. Title.
HD5660.E9K83   658.31'52'094   79-21415
ISBN 0-03-052386-9

Published in 1980 by Praeger Publishers
CBS Educational and Professional Publishing
A Division of CBS, Inc.
521 Fifth Avenue, New York, New York 10017 U.S.A.

© 1980 by Praeger Publishers

0123456789   038   987654321

Printed in the United States of America

To My Wife and Family

CONTENTS

LIST OF TABLES   x
LIST OF FIGURES   xi

Chapter

1 INTRODUCTION   1

   Statement of the Problem   1
   Definitions and Concepts   2
   Research Design, Methodology, and Strategy   6
   Conclusion   9
   Notes   10

2 HISTORY OF WORKERS' PARTICIPATION IN THE
   UNITED STATES AND EUROPE   11

   Introduction   11
   Workers' Participation in the United States:
      An Historical Overview   11
   Workers' Participation in Western Europe:
      An Historical Overview   18
   Conclusion   24
   Notes   25

3 CO-DETERMINATION IN THE FEDERAL REPUBLIC
   OF GERMANY   28

   Introduction   28
   Co-determination Laws of 1951 and 1956   28
   Works Constitution Act of 1952   31
   Co-determination Act of 1976   36
   Conclusion   39
   Notes   40

4 INDUSTRIAL DEMOCRACY IN THE BENELUX
   COUNTRIES AND SCANDINAVIA   41

   The Netherlands   41
   Belgium   45
   Luxembourg   45
   Norway   46
   Denmark   47

Sweden		47
Conclusion		48
Notes		49

5 OTHER WEST EUROPEAN CO-DETERMINATION
  REQUIREMENTS AND PROPOSALS | 51

United Kingdom	51
The European Economic Community	54
France	60
Austria	61
Ireland	62
Italy	62
Conclusion	62
Notes	63

6 EUROPEAN COMPARATIVE ANALYSIS | 65

7 WORKERS' PARTICIPATION IN NONDEMOCRATIC
  SOCIETIES | 72

Yugoslavia	72
Peru	75
Conclusion	78
Notes	78

8 ANALYSIS OF CO-DETERMINATION EFFECTS | 80

Introduction	80
Union Power	80
Co-determination: A Means to Reduce Union Power?	82
Stalemates and Compromises?	83
Workers and Co-determination	85
White Collar Workers Bypassed	88
Competency of Workers' Representatives	89
Impact on Collective Bargaining	90
Relaxing of Tension	92
Conclusion	93
Notes	93

9 IMPLICATIONS OF CO-DETERMINATION FOR U.S.
  MULTINATIONALS AND CONCLUSIONS | 95

Introduction	95
Position of Multinational Corporations in Europe	95

Implications for the Multinationals' Operations   96
Co-determination in the United States?   100
Conclusions   109
Notes   111

BIBLIOGRAPHY   112

INDEX   124

ABOUT THE AUTHOR   127

LIST OF TABLES

Table

3.1. Graphical overview of the number and type of representatives on the supervisory board level, based on the German Co-determination Act of 1976   39

6.1. International Comparative Analysis of the Legal Requirements and Proposals Pertaining to Workers' Participation in Various West European Countries   66

8.1. Frequency of Responses to Statement 1   81

8.2. Frequency of Responses to Statement 2   85

8.3. Ranking of German Workers' Interests   86

8.4. Frequency of Responses to Statement 3   90

8.5. Frequency of Responses to Statement 4   92

9.1. Frequency of Responses to Statement 1   97

9.2. Frequency of Responses to Statement 2   98

9.3. Frequency of Responses to Question 1   105

9.4. Frequency of Responses to Statement 3   106

LIST OF FIGURES

Figure

1.1.   Tasks of U.S.-type Board of Directors   6

1.2.   Difference between two types of organizational structure at
        the corporate decision-making and policy-formulating levels
        of the organization   7

3.1.   Requirements of the German Co-determination Law of 1951   30

3.2.   Organizational structure and election process of decision-
        making boards at Hoesch AG   32

3.3.   Information flow at Hoesch AG   33

3.4.   Requirements of the German Works Constitution Act of
        1952: Example for a public stock company with 12 super-
        visory board members   35

3.5.   Overview of the statutory organizational design of the super-
        visory and management board level for an organization
        statisfying the German Co-determination Act of 1976   38

4.1.   Structure of a Dutch organization   44

5.1.   Design of the supervisory and management board structure
        of an organization subject to the European Company Statute   58

1

INTRODUCTION

STATEMENT OF THE PROBLEM

Workers' participation at the board of directors' level, also called co-determination, originated immediately after World War II in the Federal Republic of Germany. Since then, movements have been launched in other countries as well to increase the influence of workers on the decision-making processes within the corporation. A more democratic form of decision making is demanded by a majority of the workers. This changing philosophy in society requires that employees be treated "as people" instead of "as objects." Closely related is the notion that labor and capital should occupy equal places in the organizational structure. The interests of the employee are related to those of the organization. Many policy decisions have far-reaching consequences for employees, as a result of which a certain amount of participatory management is justified.

Participatory management can be viewed from the standpoint of "protection of interests." It is clear that many interest groups are connected with the organization. Interests of the stockholders and creditors are protected by law, and the government is in charge of the public interest. However, the employees are connected with the fate of the organization in a special way. Their risk, although of a different nature than that of the stockholders, is, in general, larger. Employees are hit through internal organizational actions, such as reorganization, more directly than stockholders.

Employees are less able to spread their risk than shareholders, who can reduce the risk of losing their source of income by investing in several corporations. Wage levels, in most cases, do not allow employees to save a significant part of their income, and they cannot, therefore, spread the risk of losing their source of income by investing in other corporations. Generally, the employees are almost totally dependent upon the income received from

1

working for one corporation. The possibility of spreading the risk by working for several companies is not practical and in most cases is not allowed. Therefore, a protection of the employees' interest is considered justifiable.

Accéptance of the above outlined ideas in most Western European countries resulted in pressure for workers' participation at the board of directors' level. The demands by unions and workers for co-determination resulted in co-determination requirements in almost all Western European countires and in a few countries outside Europe.

Problems are related to the existing co-determination models—problems detected by all groups involved with co-determination. Unions, employees, employers' associations, and stockholders have published manuscripts explaining their specific ideas of co-determination. Condensed, they all come to the same conclusion: European co-determination models are not operating satisfactorily.

No exceptions in the statutory co-determination requirements are included pertaining to the European subsidiaries of U.S. multinational enterprises. Co-determination can affect the total world-wide operations of the multinational enterprise, including finance, marketing, personnel, and so on. Executives at the decision-making and policy-formulating levels of the U.S. multinational's headquarters must be aware of the constraints and contingencies faced as a result of statutory co-determination requirements.

To provide the executive with an understanding of the co-determination concept and its impact upon the operations of the multinational, this study is broken down into three major sections: First, a comparative analysis of the major existing co-determination requirements (see Chapters 3–6); second, an analysis of co-determination effects on the management of the U.S. multinational's subsidiary operating in a country with statutory co-determination (see Chapter 8); and third, an analysis of the implications of co-determination for the operations of the multinational enterprise (see Chapter 9). The question whether co-determination can be expected in the United States is discussed in Chapter 9.

DEFINITIONS AND CONCEPTS

Workers' participation at the board of directors' level is rather new, and most scholars describing co-determination limit themselves to providing an overview and description of the legal requirements for this type. Little empirical research on this type has been published. The most thorough and objective analysis is the 1970 study performed by Professor K. H. Biedenkopf and his associates for the German parliament (called the "Biedenkopf Report").[1]

Different names have been given to this concept of participatory management. The most common are: co-determination, employee representation, joint district councils, joint industrial councils, joint production committees, works councils, and workshop councils. This is evidence that the research on workers' participation is unstructured. Reflected, too, is the fact that various countries have different workers' participation requirements.

The concept "participative decision making" is used to describe different types of workers' participation. For most people, the working definition of participative decision making seems clear—involvement of members of an organization in the decisions of the organization. However, a review of the literature shows that there are many subtleties and distinctions. Aaron Lowin's definition is one of the clearest: "By participative decision making we mean a mode of organizational operations in which decisions as to activities are arrived at by the very persons who are to execute these decisions."[2] Lowin notes, however, that no organization operates purely on the participative decision-making principle. While Lowin's definition is clear, it also presents the ideal operational concept of participative decision making.

Almost everyone who uses the term "participative decision making" has a different understanding.[3] Johannes Schregle combined these various thoughts and showed the complexity of describing workers' participation:

> Workers' participation has become a magic word in many countries. Yet almost everyone who employs the term thinks of something different. There are people that feel that workers' participation is the panacea for solving most labor–management relations problems and it will even become the underlying concept of the future society. Some people use the term as a synonym for what they call industrial democracy. Still others use it as a battle cry for uprooting the present system of ownership and management of the economy. Again for others it is more a tool of applied psychology to be used to counteract the dehumanization of industrial work. Still others employ the term "participation" with regard to specific procedures, for instance the consultation machinery in an enterprise, negotiation over problems of displaced workers, or profit sharing.
>
> The difficulty is that the term "workers' participation" is linked with such concepts as democracy, management rights, efficiency, human needs and moral rights and has become so loaded with emotions and ideologies that a dispassionate discussion, free from preconceived opinions and pre-established attitudes, has become extremely difficult. It is even more difficult to bring this discussion to the international level because the variety of different national practices is tremendous and participants in such a discussion are likely to argue in terms of their own national system and experience.[4]

In conclusion, anyone using the term "workers' participation" defines it in a manner that corresponds with his experience or perceived conception.

Realizing the complexity of defining participative decision making, a working definition is needed. In this study, "employees' participation" is used to include a wide variety of participation activities by employees or their representatives. These participation activities range from a far-reaching effort to include employees in the organizational decision-making processes, as in Yugoslavian enterprises, subject to a system of employee self-management, to the other end of the continuum, where employees are associated with the decision making and policy formulation in the enterprise via a works council, works committee, or enterprise committee. The functions of the latter are normally of a consultative and advisory nature without voting rights.

The word "co-determination" is in the title of this study and it is appropriate to define it here. "Co-determination" is a translation from the German word *Mitbestimmung*. A precise definition of the term co-determination is, in the first place, an exercise in semantics. Generally, *Mitbestimmung* means that workers are allowed to participate in decision making, both at the shopfloor and corporate level. Legally, West German workers have these rights. Co-determination is used here to describe a situation where employees' participation takes the form of admitting one or more employee representatives as full members to the corporate decision-making board of an organization, together with the representatives of the owners.

The concept "employee representatives" applies to those members of the enterprise work force who are directly or indirectly elected or appointed by their colleagues, with or without direct recommendation of the trade unions to represent them. "Employee representatives" can also include outsiders, in most cases trade union representatives elected directly or indirectly by the enterprise work force or appointed by the trade union.

A distinction between three types of employees in an organization needs to be made: First, the hourly paid workers or the blue collar workers, described by Imperial Chemical Industries (ICI) as "weekly staff" (in German, *Arbeiter*); second, the white collar workers, described by ICI as "monthly staff" (in German, *Angestellte*); third, the management employees at the middle and upper ranks in the hierarchy (in German, *Leitende Angestellte*). When possible, the collective term "employees," embracing the three categories, is used. A distinction between these three groupings is important because their position in the various co-determination laws varies.

The Board of Directors

Most European countries require a two-tier form of structure for the decision-making and policy-formulating board, which divides the supervisory and management functions between the supervisory board and the board of management or the board of executive directors. The supervisory board's importance is signified by its power to appoint, dismiss, and supervise the board of management. Therefore, the composition of the supervisory board has a decisive effect upon that of the board of management. The latter is responsible for the day-to-day operations of the organization. Employee representatives are usually included on the supervisory board and, depending on the legal requirement, they occupy one-third or even one-half of the seats in most European countries. Shareholders have no direct influence over the employee representatives on the board. Employee representatives have full voting freedom, and the shareholders lose part of their control over their capital investment.

In the United States the law does not require a two-tier system. Often, there is a misunderstanding about the tasks of members of a U.S.-type board of directors. The establishment of a board of directors is necessary to see that resources given to an enterprise are well managed. "It is therefore, both logical and practical that the board of directors be placed in the position of *managing* the company, or more accurately of *seeing to it* that the company is well managed."[5] Thus, Harold Koontz considers supervision as the most important task of the board of directors. The organization's board of directors must not only check upon the utilization of financial resources provided to the company by investors and creditors, but it must also look after the interests of employees, customers, the local community, retailers, suppliers, and competitors.

J. Scott Armstrong draws a distinction between primary and secondary groups affected by actions of an organization's board of directors. "A primary stakeholder is affected by the decisions of the firm and also makes some contribution to the firm. A secondary stakeholder is affected by the firm's decisions, but makes no direct contribution to the firm."[6] Examples of primary stakeholders are stockholders, employees, customers, local community, retailers, creditors, and suppliers. The organization's competitors are secondary stakeholders. The degree to which the members of the board of directors *should* feel responsible to these groups of primary and secondary stakeolders depends upon the legal requirements and/or the board members' personal feelings toward social responsibility in management.

Copeland and Towl also see a need for operating executives on the board of directors next to the controlling or supervising executives:

> It is essential that the affairs of corporations be directed with a broad perspective and a long-range point of view; it is incumbent of the board of directors to provide that perspective and breadth of view. To attain these ends, the board of directors must provide for the employment of competent operating executives, for the establishment and execution of sound, consistent policies, for maintaining the solvency of the corporation.[7]

In summary, in the United States there is by law a one-tier board, but in reality the internal structure of the board of directors is two-tier as well. Some

FIGURE 1.1. Tasks of U.S. type board of directors.

	Internal Structure
U.S Board of Directors consists of:	⎧ Supervisory of controlling executives
(Tasks: managing the company and supervision of the management)	⎨ ⎩ Operations executives

Source: Constructed by the author.

members of the board of directors are employed as operating executives, involved in the day-to-day operations of the organization. The other members of the board are involved in some kind of supervisory capacity (see Figure 1.1).

If a European structure was followed, then the group of operating executives could be called the "board of management," and the group of supervisory executives the "supervisory board" (see Figure 1.2). In the case that co-determination is required by law in the United States at some point in time, then a breakdown into groups—supervisory and management—should not provide many problems.

RESEARCH DESIGN, METHODOLOGY, AND STRATEGY

It was necessary to collect and analyze as much literature pertaining to co-determination as possible, considering that co-determination is a rather new phenomenon for scholars. These publications provided a starting point.

This study is broken down into three research-type sections, each one requiring a different type of research, ranging from literature reviews to field interviews. The literature available for each major research section varied, and this, as well as the different types of research, resulted in three separate research sections.

Historical Overview of Workers' Participation

The purpose here was to trace the history of employees' participation in Western Europe and the United States. For the sake of clarity, the history of workers' participation was traced separately for the two regions.

The literature review on workers' participation is presented chronologically. Explanations and summaries which are generally accepted or that may be reasonably inferred from the events are included. Sources of data for this

FIGURE 1.2. Difference between two types of organizational structure at the corporate decision-making and policy-formulating levels of the organization.

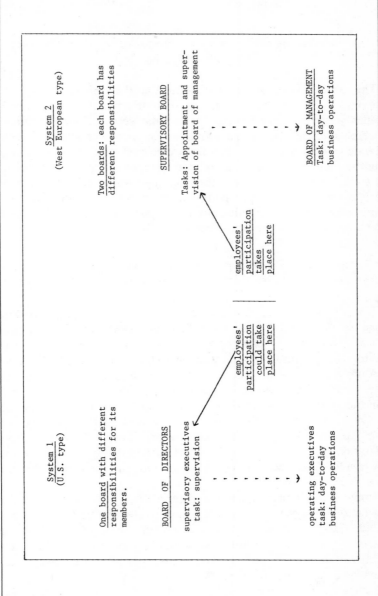

Source: Constructed by the author.

section are mostly articles, found through the use of the *International Index* (now known as the *Social Sciences and Humanities Index*), *Readers Guide to Periodical Literature* and *Business Periodicals Index*. The articles found by this method often provide leads to other sources and related articles.

Review of Contemporary Requirements Pertaining to Co-determination

The source for data on existing statutory co-determination models included a review of the literature pertaining to co-determination written in English, French, German, and Dutch. These data were collected through library research, mailings with requests for information, and various other techniques. Interviews were also conducted with government officials in various European countries and representatives of the European Economic Community in Brussels. The main purpose of the interviews was to gain a sense of what, in fact, the legal requirements pertaining to workers' participation are and to obtain explanation concerning questions which arose during the execution of the above-mentioned review of the literature.

Implications of Co-determination for Multinational Corporations and the Probability of Co-determination in the United States.

The analysis of whether or not co-determination will be required by law in some form in the United States in the near future is based on, among other sources, opinions of at least two of its major labor organizations, the AFL-CIO and the United Auto Workers. Almost no literature is available on this topic.

A similar constraint was found while evaluating the implications of co-determination for the operations of multinational enterprises doing business in countries with statutory co-determination. Little has been published, either in the United States or Europe, about the effects of co-determination upon U.S. multinationals. Publications issued by the German unions and employer federations in most cases are biased and unsupported by empirical evidence. These publications were studied and analyzed to obtain a more comprehensive view.

Studying this limited and biased material alone would not have resulted in a satisfactory analysis of the true effects of co-determination. It was necessary to include questionnaires to obtain data, which would allow a more thorough analysis. The results of a trial questionnaire mailed early in 1975 to a small number of companies in West Germany revealed that companies and their managements generally were not willing to provide written information regarding their experience and perceptions on co-determination. Co-determination and its perceived effects are highly controversial topics as they touch upon the basic principles of control and responsibility over property as a result of ownership. The author's follow-up telephone conversations with the recipients of the trial questionnaire revealed that they feared that any negative comments based on the recipients' experiences with co-determination within their company would hinder management's relationships and communication with labor, works councils, and unions. The results of these telephone conversations also indicated that executives were willing to participate in personal interviews if the identity of the firm or individual interviewed would not be revealed.

Consequently, it was decided not to use questionnaires as a mode of research, but rather to rely on personal interviews. The major disadvantages of using personal interviews are cost and small sample size, but the major advantages are the depth and quality of the material obtained. In a questionnaire, the researcher is limited in the number of questions that can be asked and in the accuracy of the answer provided by the respondent. Interviews were held with union leaders in several countries, government officials in various countries, employer representatives and employee representatives of various multinationals in Europe, representatives of employer federations in West Germany and the Netherlands, officials of the European Economic Community, and executives of U.S. multinationals.

As outlined above, with the trial questionnaire experience, it would be a breach of confidence to reveal the identity of the individuals or the firms interviewed. Only when the interviewed persons have approved the use of their name or identity is this done in this study.[8]

CONCLUSION

In this chapter, the foundation of the study has been outlined and the definitions of the concepts have been set forth.

Employees' participation is used here to include a wide variety of participation activities by employees or their representatives. Co-determination is used to describe a situation where employees' participation takes the form of admitting one or more employer representatives as full members to the corporate decision-making board, together with the representatives of the owners.

There appears to be a difference between the U.S. and Western Europe type of corporate decision-making boards. A comparison, however, reveals that both types are almost identical and have similar responsibilities.

The research design of this study is broken down into three sections, in which each required a different type of research, ranging from literature reviews to field interviews. The mode of research was determined by the availability of literature pertaining to co-determination.

NOTES

1. See K.H. Biedenkopf, et al., *Mitbestimmung Im Unternehmen*, Deutscher Bundestag, 6. Wahlperiode, VI/334, 1970.

2. Aaron Lowin, "Participative Decision Making: A Model, Literature Critique and Prescriptions for Research," *Organizational Behavior and Human Performance* 3 (February 1968): 69.

3. See also: Michael R. Cooper and Michael T. Wood, "Effects of Member Participation and Commitment in Group Decision Making on Influence, Satisfaction and Decision Riskiness," *Journal of Applied Psychology* 59 (1974): 127; Raymond E. Miles and J.B. Ritchie, "Participative Management: Quality vs. Quantity," *California Management Review* 13 (Summer 1971): 48–49; Rensis Likert, *New Patterns of Management* (New York: McGraw-Hill, 1961): 242.

4. Johannes Schregle, "Forms of Participation in Management," *Industrial Relations* 9 (February 1970): 117.

5. Harold Koontz, *The Board of Directors and Effective Management* (New York: McGraw-Hill, 1967), p. 1.

6. J. Scott Armstrong, "Social Irresponsibility in Management," *Journal of Business Research* 5 (September 1977): 185–213.

7. Melvin T. Copeland and Andrew R. Towl, *The Board of Directors and Business Management* (Andover, Mass.: Andover Press, 1974), pp. 3–4.

8. The interviews with the persons and institutions, as outlined above, took place during seven individual research trips to Europe between July 1975 and February 1979.

2

HISTORY OF WORKERS' PARTICIPATION IN THE UNITED STATES AND EUROPE

INTRODUCTION

The history of employees' participation in Western Europe and the United States will be analyzed in this chapter. For the sake of clarity, the history of workers' participation is discussed separately for the two regions. The analysis is presented chronologically with explanations and summaries that are generally accepted or that may be inferred from the events. Most of the articles used for this chapter were found through the use of the *International Index* (now known as the *Social Sciences and Humanities Index*), *Readers Guide to Periodical Literature*, and *Business Periodicals Index*. Articles found by this method often provided leads to other related articles.

WORKERS' PARTICIPATION IN THE UNITED STATES: AN HISTORICAL OVERVIEW

1898–1915

In the United States, the earliest known form of employee representation took place at the Filene Department Store around 1898 in Boston.[1] This gave the employees control of the cafeteria and certain employee funds. Later they were given the power to amend or adopt administrative store rules by vote. The proprietor had the power to veto proposals, but his could be overturned if two-thirds of the employees voted to do so. In 1901 the employees were given the right to elect a board to handle employee grievances.[2]

In the United States, the first known shop committee was organized by Mr. H. F. J. Porter, vice-president and general manager of the Nerst Lamp Company, Pittsburg, Pennsylvania in 1904.[3] This committee was set up by Mr. Porter to bring a cohesiveness between management and employees and consisted of representatives elected by employees plus a company official appointed by management. The shop committee had no power, but it was a vehicle for better communication of employee desires.

John Leitch carried employee representation to the ultimate. He developed a plan calling for a house of representatives to represent workers, a senate to represent foremen, and a cabinet to represent top management.[4] For a proposal to become law it had to pass all three bodies. Leitch's plan was adopted in 1913 by the Packard Piano Company where it met with success. No other information concerning the fate of the Leitch plan at the Packard Piano Company was uncovered other than the fact that Derber mentioned its success.

After an unsuccessful strike for union recognition by employees of the Colorado Fuel and Iron Company, John D. Rockefeller, Jr. offered a plan for employee representation, which was accepted and became effective on October 2, 1915.[5] Colorado Fuel and Iron Company was the first known large company in the United States to adopt an employee representation plan. Most commonly known as the Rockefeller plan, it was also called the Colorado plan. This plan called for an election of representatives by the workers to attend district conferences.[6] These conferences consisted of an equal number of workers' representatives and company representatives. Matters relative to the interests of both parties were discussed. The company's president could convene joint district conferences if he so desired. Annually, a joint conference of all the districts met to discuss mutual interests.

During the interval of 1898 to 1915, other companies had employee representation plans in operation, but no known literature analyzing these plans is available. The common denominator was that they were initiated by management and were not established by government regulation.

1916–1930

Various agencies of the U.S. government had set up shop committees throughout private industry to aid the war effort (1917–1919).[7] During World War I, unions in the United States had agreed not to strike, and the U.S. government had taken a stand not to force union recognition on employers.[8] Between 1918 and early 1919, 225 individual shop committees were established in 176 companies, employing a total of around 450,000 workers.[9]

By 1919 Leitch's employee representation plan, as outlined earlier, consisting of a house of representatives, a senate, and a cabinet, was adopted by 20 companies. Among these firms were the Atlantic Refining Company and the American Multigraph Company, both in Cleveland, Ohio.[10] Although the Leitch plan was in use, it did not spread because its operation was somewhat cumbersome and impractical.

The number of conflicts between unions and shop committees rose with the growth of labor unions. In 1919, the Western Union Telegraph Company's shop committees actively participated to defeat a move toward recognizing a union.[11] The union movement in the steel industry was also conflicting with shop committees.[12] Because of these events, leaders of the steel union movement persuaded the 1919 American Federation of Labor (AFL) convention in Atlantic City, New Jersey to condemn both shop committees and employee representation plans. Later, in 1919, at the First Industrial Conference, Samuel Gompers, president of the AFL, announced that organized labor would fight the shop committee system to the end.[13] However, by the early 1920s, the shop committee system had secured itself "in the iron and steel industries, machine manufacturing, coal and iron mining, textiles, food products, and public service corporations."[14]

From 1916 to 1939 the battle lines were drawn between employees and trade unions. The 1920s were marked by confrontations between trade unions and shop committees. These were the years in which the U.S. worker chose between working with management or with trade unions.

1930–1939

During the depression in the 1930s, the unions made strong gains in the United States because of the support given by the New Deal administration. Most union gains were at the expense of employee representation plans. The biggest blow to employee representation plans came with the passage of the National Labor Relations Act of 1935. This act, more commonly known as the Wagner Act, denied the employer a role in employee groups and promoted unionism.

A significant event occurred in 1938 involving Joseph Scanlon, one of the leaders in a union representing workers in an economically failing Ohio steel company. In an effort to continue operation, Scanlon and other union leaders agreed with management on a plan for joint labor-management committees to solicit employee suggestions on how to increase efficiency, reduce production costs, and eliminate waste.[15] The rewards for workers to participate in these efforts included steady employment, better working conditions, productivity bonuses, and higher wages. The Scanlon plan was a success; after implementation, operating costs were dramatically reduced and the company became profitable again. Clinton Golden, the Steelworkers Union's vice-president, called Joseph Scanlon to their national headquarters to help other companies. As a result, Scanlon designed plans for about 50 other companies. The fundamentals of the Scanlon plan were: (1) bonuses to workers for reductions in labor costs, and (2) the use of "production committees" to gather and implement suggestions.[16]

Under the piecework bonus system, veteran workers were reluctant to show trainees shortcuts. This problem was alleviated by the Scanlon plan because the plan's aim was to increase bonuses for everyone's benefit. The Scanlon plan also does away with the problem of labor pacing itself in order not to have its normal output rate increased. The Scanlon plan works because it does not deal with grievances or wage problems. The plan also unifies management and labor to reach a common goal. The Scanlon plan provided a new method for management and labor to work together.

1940–1977

The United States needed the full cooperation of labor to make the transition from peace to war, since it was not prepared for World War II. Early in 1942, the War Production Board[17] asked that joint committees be voluntarily organized in plants involved in the war effort with the objective of increasing production.[18] Over 800 plants, with approximately 2 million employees, had established labor-management committees three months after the Board's request.[19] The accomplishments of these committees were encouraging. In a 1942 *Time* article, the following improvements were listed: at the end of only one month's operation of production committees, a Westinghouse Electric plant in Cleveland, Ohio increased production by 17 percent; at Douglas Aircraft, the suggestions of employees resulted in a saving of 2,000 man-hours a day; the Continental Roll and Steel Foundry of Chicago increased production 20 percent through the adoption of 200 suggestions submitted by workers; the Elgin Watch Company had a 65 percent rise of output over its production quota in its fuse plant; in Aurora, Illinois at the Independent Pneumatic Tool Company, production increased 21 percent.[20]

In July 1945, approximately 3,200 plants reported active joint production committees. In January 1948, the U.S. Bureau of Labor Statistics mailed questionnaires to these 3,200 plants to determine if the joint production committees were still functioning. Only 944 replies out of the 1,272 questionnaires returned were usable. Of these, 287 reported functioning joint production committees. The major reason for the discontinuation of the joint production committees was a lack of interest among workers.[21] U.S. labor, unlike its European counterparts, did not seek to gain a voice in management. U.S. labor accepted big business and was more concerned with wages and related benefits than sharing decision making with management.

In 1948, Professors Coch and French conducted an experiment on workers and decision making. It was carried out at the Harwood Manufacturing Corporation in Marion, Virginia.[22] Up to the time of this experiment, the company had noticed that workers' production had dropped off after job changes. Four groups were used to study the effect of workers' participation and production outputs. One was designated as the control group and was permitted no participation. The other three were experimental groups. One experimental group was given representative participation, and the other two were given total participation. The experiment showed that participation was directly linked to the production of workers, employee relations, and job satisfaction.

In 1956, Morse and Reimer published their results of an experiment conducted in an industrial organization.[23] It was designed to study the effects of decision making upon personal satisfaction and productivity. The experiment used four similar clerical groups in one organization and introduced two methods of changes. Two of the groups received an increase in power in the decision-making process of the company. The other two groups saw management's power increased in regard to decision making. The experiment measured the relationships of decision making, satisfaction, and productivity prior to the experiment. Supervisors were trained for six months prior to the beginning of the experiment. The experiment lasted for one year. Measurements were taken during the experiment and at its conclusion. Some of the findings were:

The desired differences in the allocation of the decision-making process between the groups were achieved.

Personal satisfaction increased significantly with increases in decision making. It was also observed that personal satisfaction decreased significantly with decreases in decision making.

Under both methods of decision making, productivity increased. It was found that a greater increase in productivity was achieved by the clerical groups which had their decision making decreased.

In 1965, Patchen released the results of questionnaires returned by 834 employees working for the Tennessee Valley Authority.[24] The findings showed that an active participation program leads to the employee identifying with the company and management. It was also found that success of workers' participation is not dependent on the degree of job satisfaction. The participation program is only successful if the employees feel that their suggestions are genuinely being taken into consideration.

The results of an experiment conducted by French, Kay, and Meyer were released in 1966.[25] It involved the General Electric Company and consisted of two groups. During appraisal interviews, one group participated extensively and the other group's participation was restricted. The extensive participation group was instructed to write out goals for future performance and the methods for achieving these goals. The extensive participation group had two weeks to bring these plans to a planning session. In the restricted participation group, the manager told the subordinates to come back in two weeks. The manager determined their goals and methods of achievement. In the planning session, the subordinates in the extensive participation group set their own goals, and they were only changed if it was deemed necessary. In the planning session, subordinates in the restricted participation group were assigned goals and only permitted a minimum of input. Results of this experiment showed that generally increased participation improved relations between subordinate and manager. Decreased participation did not result in the anticipated undesirable consequences.

In 1969, the results of the operation of the Scanlon plan in the Parker Pen Company, Pfaudler Company, and the Atwood Vacuum Machine Company were analyzed by Lesieur and Puckett.[26] The Atwood Vacuum Machine Company operated under the Scanlon plan for 14 years in six of its plants. Atwood Vacuum Machine Company supplied automotive parts to automotive manufacturers. The Scanlon plan produced impressive results at Atwood; for example, for 14 years, annual bonuses from 5 percent to 20 percent of the annual payroll had been distributed. Throughout 187 operating periods (a period consisted of four weeks), bonuses occurred in 163 periods and the greatest monthly bonus reached 26 percent. Another interesting result of the Scanlon plan was that over 25,000 suggestions had been submitted by workers.

The Parker Pen Company operated under the Scanlon plan in its manu-facturing division in Janesville, Wisconsin for 14 years. The plan produced impressive results. Annual bonuses ranged from a low of 5.5 percent to a high of 20 percent. The Scanlon plan was in operation for 168 months, and bonuses were paid in 142 of them. During the 14 years, bonuses were found to interrelate with division profits. The success of the Scanlon plan is even more remarkable when it is recognized that Parker operated in a highly price-conscious market. For example, the company's Jotter ball pen's price of $1.98 did not change from 1955 through 1969. This is an indication of an increase in worker efficiency.

The Pfaudler Company operated under the Scanlon plan for 17 years. The company, located in Rochester, New York produced chemical and food processing equipment. Annual bonuses ranged from a low of 3 percent to a high of 17.5 percent of annual wages. Through 204 operating months, bonuses were paid in 179 of them.

In 1973, results of another study of the Scanlon plan were released.[27] Managers of 18 manufacturing companies which had operated under the Scanlon plan were interviewed. Ten were still using the Scanlon plan and eight had discontinued it. Managers first were asked to rate managers on their own level, the manager's subordinates, and rank-and-file employees on a seven point scale. Each manager was asked to rate such qualities as judgment and responsibility. In the second part of the questionnaire the manager was asked to rate statements concerning workers' participation. Results showed that managers of companies which had abandoned the Scanlon plan did not have as much confidence in their employees as managers in organizations still operating under the Scanlon plan. Managers with favorable attitudes toward workers' participation were in organizations currently using the Scanlon plan. The authors noted that just because managers had less favorable attitudes, it did not mean it was the reason the Scanlon plan had failed.

Ruh and White released their findings concerning participative management in December 1973:[28]

> In general, the advocates of participative management view the conditions of modern industrial life as frustrating the higher order of needs of most employees. Eliminating this frustration by increasing employee participation in decision making is seen as providing the organization with previously untapped energy or perhaps redirected energy, which had been previously redirected against the organization. Furthermore, high levels of participation in decision making are assumed to contribute to favorable responses for all, or at least, most employees.[29]

Over 2,750 workers from 19 plants in the Midwest were questioned to test these views. Participative decision making positively affected motivation, the worker's identification with the company, and job involvement.

In 1974, Alutto and Acito published their findings relating to participative decision making in a New York manufacturing company.[30] The task of identifying those decisions in which they desired to participate was given to 80 workers. The workers were also asked to state if they participated in these decisions presently. Results indicated that workers who felt that they were not participating in decision making identified less with the company, felt a greater amount of tension from their jobs, and were dissatisfied with almost all facets of the organization. The degree of discontent was directly correlated with the degree of perceived lack of participation by the workers.

Krishan, in 1974, published the findings of a questionnaire distributed to managers in a Midwest industrial area.[31] One of the questions concerned allowing employees to vote on relocation of a plant. An overwhelming majority of 81 percent felt that employees should not have a vote on the relocation site.

Since 1940, worker participation in decision making has not been widely used except during World War II. Management does not feel any need or great desire to give workers a larger share in decision making. On the other hand, there is no major perceptible demand by U.S. workers today for participation in the decision-making process.[32]

WORKERS' PARTICIPATION IN WESTERN EUROPE:
AN HISTORICAL OVERVIEW

Before World War I

A specific date for the first occurrence in Western Europe of workers' participation in management is unknown. Authors generally pinpoint the beginning around the 1880s or 1890s. Frederic Meyers states that the first joint councils were organized in France in 1885.[33] He also notes that legislation was passed in 1891 in Germany which provided for voluntary councils, but he does not cite his sources. There are two major reasons why workers' participation did not spread: first, strong autocratic managements existed in industry at that time; second, the majority of the workers were unprepared to take the responsibility of decision making. Workers' participation was to lay dormant until World War I.

1914–1918

The nations involved in World War I increased production to the fullest to aid their war efforts, and the rights of workers were forgotten. This led to labor unrest during the war. The British government realized that labor turmoil could seriously hinder the war effort, and in October 1916, Prime Minister Lloyd George appointed a commission, known as the British Reconstruction Committee on Relations between Employers and Employed, to study the problems of labor and to make recommendations concerning improvements in industrial relations.[34] In time, this committee came to be known as the Whitley committee, after its chairman, John Whitley. In 1917, the Whitley committee recommended that national industrial councils be set up in each industry.[35] These national councils were to organize district and local councils and they were to consist of employees and employers. Their objectives were to include a fuller utilization in determining methods and conditions pertaining to work and to propose legislation which would affect themselves.

In late 1917, the British War Cabinet adopted the idea of joint industrial councils as proposed by the Whitley committee.[36] The minister of labor had the power to officially recognize or not recognize a joint industrial council.[37] A joint industrial council was recognized if it was deemed to be representative of that particular industry. After recognition, the joint industrial council was considered by the British government as the official body to consult in matters pertaining to that particular industry.

1918–1923

After the revolution of 1918 in Germany, councils appeared with the objective to demobilize Germany and to socialize production.[38] This was an attempt by German labor to prevent the rise of prewar conditions and the hope for industrial democracy. It was part of the social struggle which sought to eradicate autocratic management of industry. The German government passed legislation in 1918 which provided for workers' committees. The latter were only to represent the social rights of the workers.

A 1920 works council law in Germany called for the election of works councils in all companies employing 20 or more persons.[39] It also stated that one or two employees from the works council may sit on the board of directors.

The German factory inspection service[40] concluded in 1921 that works councils and employers were, indeed, working together and that basically the works councils were conservative.[41] Only the radical works councils functioned with difficulties.

Legislation was passed in 1919 in Austria which made works councils mandatory in all organizations employing 20 or more workers.[42] It provided employees with the power to demand monthly meetings with the employer. Works councils were also given the power to elect two representatives to the board of directors.

In Austria, a chambers of labor (a government agency to deal with labor) was established by law in 1920 which covered all wage earners.[43] The institution of this new body in effect nullified the joint industrial councils. The workers considered the chambers of labor a better instrument than the joint industrial councils to serve their interests.

After World War I, Belgium faced problems of high unemployment, lack of machinery, and financing. The industrial councils, instituted to cope with these problems, were successful as unemployment was virtually nonexistent by the summer of 1920.[44]

In Czechoslovakia, legislation was passed in 1921 which required works councils in other than state owned factories employing 30 or more employees.[45] They were similar to those in other European countries. Findings of the Czecho-Slovak Factory Inspection Service[46] in 1922 revealed that only a few factories had works councils. Workers felt that the shop stewards could best represent them and that they did not utilize their rights.[47]

A 1923 report on industrial councils in England showed that 73 joint industrial councils were organized but 15 had become defunct.[48] Three reasons for failure were cited: ineffective organization, wage problems, and conflicts of interest on councils. The conclusion was that the councils were successful on the whole.

1924–1939

By 1924, labor's clamor for participation in organizational decision making had crested and was falling. Most governments and industries were unwilling to give labor any real voice in decisions. This was evident at the International Congress on Social Policy in Prague, 1924, when the French delegation rejected mandatory works councils on the grounds that the workers were not ready for it.[49] Between 1924 and 1939, little occurred in connection with workers' participation in Western Europe. Time had eroded much of the zeal behind attempts to attain more power for the workers, and their attention was drawn from the new ideological concepts toward more pressing problems such as inflation and wages. Another problem was the legislation itself. It had been passed in watered down forms throughout Western Europe and created organizations of workers with virtually no powers and vague functions. Inability of the workers to utilize fully the little power that was given to them by law also caused the concept of workers' participation to wane.

Between 1924 and 1939 there were two noteworthy occurrences in Western Europe. The first dealt with the Netherlands in 1932, and the second concerned the status of the Whitley councils of 1938. In 1932, legislation was passed in the Netherlands providing for the establishment of industrial councils.[50] The law did not set any specific guidelines as to what industries should have industrial councils. It stated only that the industrial councils were to advise governmental bodies. The councils' members were to be appointed by employers' associations and workers' unions. An equal number were to be appointed by both parties. The councils also had the power to settle the problems of management and labor.

In 1939, an article appeared by the U.S. consul in London, Harry Carlson, who had examined the Whitley councils through 1938.[51] He concluded that the Whitley councils were successful and attributed this to several factors: the British government sent out information about the Whitley councils and then requested labor and employers to consider the Whitley report's recommendations; it also set up a department specifically to deal with the implementation of the Whitley plan; the councils were divided on national, district, and local levels, which allowed the levels to support each other; and the last, but most important reason was the regular meetings of the councils.

As noted previously, the period between 1924 and 1939 was marked by management's opposition to workers' participation and labor's lack of interest. Another reason for the decline in workers' participation in management was Adolph Hitler's rise to power in Germany in 1933. Workers' participation was abolished by the Nazis. In the late 1930s, Germany's occupation of Austria and Czechoslovakia led to the abolishment of workers' participation in these two countries.

1940–1949

The Director-General of Ordnance Factories in Great Britain decided to institute "joint production consultative advisory committees" in the Royal ordnance factories, and representatives of both the unions and of the British government formulated a plan for these committees in 1942.[52] The committees' power was of an advisory nature, and the objective was to increase production and to make production more efficient. The agreement allowed a maximum of ten workers' representatives and a maximum of ten management representatives. Late in 1944, the parliamentary secretary to the Ministry of Production stated that the nearly 500 production committees established in the British war factories had been successful.[53]

Through a decree in 1944, the French Committee of National Liberation organized joint production committees and a national committee in the aircraft industry.[54] An ordinance on February 22, 1945 established works' committees in all industries employing at least 100 workers.[55] The power to impose works' committees in companies not specifically covered by the law was established. Works committees were given access to all company records, control of social programs, and were only required to keep production information secret.[56]

Changes also took place in Belgium concerning workers' participation. In 1945, the Belgian government recognized the joint committees that were in operation in Belgium and set up guidelines for them.[57] By law, the government gave the joint committees the rights to establish general pay scales, to discuss employment conditions, to recommend legislation, and to encourage training programs. This law also provided that a joint committee could request a royal order to make its decision binding.[58]

In 1945, the British army took over the steel industry in Germany and gave labor some of the management powers.[59] On January 17, 1947, the German steel industry began operating under the control of the Steel Trustee Association, a German group established by the British North German Iron and Steel Control Board.[60] The industry was divided into 24 companies controlled by an 11-man board. Five members were chosen by the German Federation of Labor (DGB) and five represented management. On the latter group, three represented old stockholders, one new management, and one the public. The eleventh member was appointed by the Steel Trustee Association and served as chairman.

In April of 1947, Austrian legislation was passed establishing works committees with basically the same powers as those in France.[61] The primary difference between the French and the Austrian law was the Austrian works committees' right to recommend change, and if the recommendation was not followed, then the works committee could ask the government to rule on the recommendation, and the government's decision was final. The works committee had the right to have two elected representatives on the board of directors if the company was a joint stock company. The representatives were to be equal in power and to have the same duties as other members of the board of directors.

The governments of Denmark and Italy required works councils as well by 1947. In Italy, the General Confederation of Industry and the General Confederation of Labor had agreed to works committees in organizations employing over 25 workers.[62] Their expressed duty was to advise management. A 1947 agreement between the Danish Employers' Confederation and the Confederation of Danish Trade Unions allowed works committees in enterprises employing 25 workers or more. They could be established if the employer or a majority of the workers desired one.[63]

The 1940s were a repeat of the occurrences in the years during and directly following World War I. In both wars it had become necessary to consult labor to improve war production. After World War II ended, legislation was passed in most countries giving labor a voice in management. The new legislation was a step toward democracy. It was an affirmation of freedom after the years of German occupation. The movement in Germany resulted from workers feeling that the industrialists had supported Hitler. They wanted a voice in industry to prevent any similar reoccurrences.

1950–1977

On May 21, 1951, a law was passed in West Germany in which employees' participation in the decision-making process of companies in the iron, steel, and mining industries was required.[64] This law, in English commonly referred to as the co-determination law, called for a board of managers to be responsible for the operations of the company under the direct supervision of the supervisory board.[65] The supervisory board consisted of an equal number of representatives of employers and employees and one impartial member. The impartial member could not be an employer or employee of the company, financially linked with it, or a representative of a labor union or employers' federation.

Labor and management were not satisfied with the requirements in this 1951 co-determination law. Industrialists were against the idea of unions nominating labor representatives who did not work for the company. Nor was the co-determination law exactly what labor wanted. Labor's original plan included:

1.   A "Federal Economic Council" (half management and half workers) to advise the government on economic activities

2.   "State Industrial Councils" for state government
3.   "Economic Chambers" to regulate industry
4.   The board of directors to be half management and half labor
5.   A "uniform works council law" for co-determination on the plant level[66]

Labor wanted co-determination in West Germany for several reasons. They were not about to relinquish workers' representation on the supervisory boards of the iron, coal, and steel companies as the Allies gave up their control over the industry. Co-determination was an attempt to socialize the power that controls industry without socializing the ownership of industry. It was also a foundation to rebuild union power and a reflection of the lack of faith that government could regulate industry instead of industry regulating government.

On October 11, 1952, co-determination was extended to almost all West German industries.[67] Labor was unhappy because this new federal law was weaker than many of the local laws in existence. Since the federal law superseded all local laws, labor did not feel that it had really won. There were also other reasons for labor's dissatisfaction with the 1952 co-determination law. Labor objected to the separate election of works council representatives by hourly workers and salaried workers. It also objected to receiving only one-third labor representation on the supervisory board as opposed to the one-half labor representation it advocated.[68]

In 1960, Delperee reviewed the work of joint committees in Belgium.[69] He stated that since 1949, there had been over 1,000 royal orders making joint committees' decisions legal and binding. He also pointed out that 75 industrial joint councils were in operation covering nearly all Belgian employees and employers.[70] Joint committees and industrial councils were functioning well and they were an important tool of Belgian labor and management.

In 1960, one of the first important experiments concerning workers' participation in decision making occurred in Western Europe. The purpose was to repeat the 1948 experiment of Coch and French in the United States.[71] The purpose of this duplication was to see if the results of the experiments would differ based on a cultural difference. In this experiment, participation referred to "a process in which two or more parties influence each other in making certain plans, policies and decisions.... It is restricted to decisions that have future effects on all those making the decisions and on those represented by them."[72]

The experiment took place in a manufacturing plant in a small town in Norway. The factory employed 1,600 people, 1,300 of them classified workers. The experiment involved the factory's footwear department and it focused on nine four-man groups that were going to have job transitions. Four groups were control groups and five were experimental. The five experimental groups were further broken down—two were permitted "moderate partici-pation" and three "weak participation."[73] Results indicated that the two experimental groups permitted "moderate participation" were able to achieve the average rate of production in a shorter time interval than normal.

In 1962, Harriet Holter conducted a study in Norway and questioned 628 nonsupervisory personnel from 18 companies at random.[74] The study revealed that nonsupervisors wanted more voice in deciding the company's welfare but did not individually want to make decisions alongside executives. In general, the workers wanted more control in decisions pertaining to their jobs.

In June of 1966, legislation was passed in France to amend the ordinance of February 22, 1945.[75] The ordinance of 1945 established works committees in all industries employing 100 or more employees in France. These works committees had access to all company records, control of social programs, and were required only to keep production information secret. The 1966 legislation applies to organizations with more than 300 workers. Management has to advise the works committee of any changes in employment or production. The head of the organization has to supply the works committee every three months with information about production, employment, and the actions taken on works committees' proposals.

Workers' participation in decision making has enjoyed a resurgence in Western Europe during the last several years.[76] In Sweden, workers were recently given the right to audit the company's books. In the Netherlands, employers are not allowed to close financially troubled plants without conferring first with works councils. In Norway, the employees may determine if they want to elect representatives to the board of directors. In France, a national commission has recently proposed that workers be permitted one-third representation on a company's board of directors and it points out that the workers today are better educated than their predecessors and should, therefore, be given a voice in management.

CONCLUSION

In this chapter the history of workers' participation in the United States and Western Europe was outlined. For both regions the first known occurrence of workers' participation was around the 1890s. Shop committees and works councils were set up throughout private industry in the United States and Western European nations to increase production to the fullest during World Wars I and II.

Since 1945, workers' participation in decision making has not been widely used in the United States. Management does not feel any need or great desire to give workers a larger share in decision making. On the other hand, workers do not place co-determination high on their list of priorities.

In Western Europe, the promulgation of the West German Co-determination Law of 1951 marked the true beginning of employees' participation in decision making and it is strongly entrenched in Western Europe.

NOTES

1. Milton Derber, "The Idea of Industrial Democracy in America: 1915–1935," *Labor History* 8 (Winter 1967): 5.

2. *Ibid.*

3. C.E. French, "The Shop Committee in the U.S.," *John Hopkins University Studies in Historical and Political Science* 41 (1923): 15.

4. Derber, op. cit., p. 6.

5. French, op. cit., p. 17.

6. The working details of the Rockefeller or Colorado plan are from: U.S. Department of Labor, "Colorado Fuel and Iron Company Industrial Representation Plan," *Monthly Labor Review* 1 (December 1915): 13. Authors were not identified in any of the U.S. Department of Labor's publications and articles cited in this book.

7. French, op. cit., p. 26.

8. Ibid., p. 24.

9. Ibid., p. 29.

10. Ibid., p. 17.

11. Ibid., p. 31.

12. Ibid.

13. Ibid.

14. Ibid., p. 29.

15. The data of the Scanlon plan are from: Russell Davenport, "Enterprise for Everyman," *Fortune* XLI (January 1950): 50–58; Carl F. Frost, John H. Wakely, and Robert A. Ruh, *The Scanlon Plan for Organization Development: Identity, Participation and Equity* (East Lansing, Mich.: Michigan State University Press), 1974.

16. Davenport, op. cit., p. 58.

17. The War Production Board coordinated the production efforts of private industries during World War II.

18. "Joint Labor-Management Committees in the United States," *International Labour Review* 45 (May 1942): 554.

19. "Workers Help Management," *Time* 39 (June 15, 1942): 81.

20. Ibid.

21. Frank McElroy and Alexander Moros, "Joint Production Committees, January 1948," *Monthly Labor Review* 67 (August 1948): 123, 124.

22. The information about the Harwood Manufacturing Corporation experiment is from: L. Coch and J.R.P. French, Jr., "Overcoming Resistance to Change," *Human Relations* 1 (1948): 512–32.

23. The data of this experiment are from: N. Morse and E. Reimer, "The Experimental Change of a Major Organizational Variable," *Journal of Abnormal and Social Psychology* 52 (1956):120–29.

24. M. Patchen, "Labor-Management Consultation at TVA: Its Impact on Employees," *Administrative Science Quarterly* 10 (1965): 149–74.

25. J.R.P. French, E. Kay, and H.H. Meyer, "Participation and the Appraisal System," *Human Relations* 19 (1966): 3–19.

26. The following data are from F.G. Lesieur and E.S. Puckett, "The Scanlon Plan Has Proved Itself," *Harvard Business Review* XLVII (October 1969): 109–18.

27. The following data are from: R. Ruh, et al., "Management Attitudes and the Scanlon Plan," *Industrial Relations* 12 (October 1973): 282–88.

28. R. Ruh and J. White, "Effects of Personnel Values on the Relationship Between Participation and Job Attitudes," *Administrative Science Quarterly* 18 (December 1973): 506–14.

29. Ibid., p. 506.

30. J. Alutto and F. Acito, "Decisional Participation and Sources of Job Satisfaction: A Study of Manufacturing Personnel," *Academy of Management Journal* 17 (March 1974): 160–67.

31. R. Krishan, "Democratic Participation in Decision Making by Employees in American Corporations," *Academy of Management Journal* 17 (June 1974): 339–47.

32. "Co-determination: When Workers Help Manage," *Business Week* (July 14, 1975): 133.

33. Frederic Meyers, "Workers' Control of Industry in Europe," *The South-Western Social Science Quarterly* 39 (June 1958): 102.

34. U.S. Department of Labor, "Final Report on Joint Industrial Councils, Great Britain," *Monthly Labor Review* 7 (December 1918): 1513.

35. U.S. Department of Labor, "Proposed Joint Standing Industrial Councils in Great Britain," *Monthly Labor Review* 5 (September 1917): 543.

36. _____, "British Government's Attitude on Joint Standing Industrial Councils," *Monthly Labor Review* 6 (March 1918): 573.

37. _____, "Constitution on Functions of a Joint Industrial Council," *Monthly Labor Review* 7 (August 1918): 296.

38. _____, "Labor Unrest in Germany," *Monthly Labor Review* 12 (April 1921): 871.

39. _____, "German Works Council Law," *Monthly Labor Review* 10 (November 1919): 1538.

40. Although the German factory service was never defined, it can be reasonably assumed that it was a German government agency that annually inspected the factories.

41. U.S. Department of Labor, "Operation of German Works Councils," *Monthly Labor Review* 16 (March 1923): 7.

42. _____, "Austrian Law Establishing Works Councils," *Monthly Labor Review* 9 (September 1919): 741.

43. _____, "Austrian Law Establishing Chambers of Labor," *Monthly Labor Review* 10 (June 1920): 1495.

44. Henry de Man, "Industrial Councils in Belgium," *Survey* 44 (July 3, 1920): 478–82.

45. U.S. Department of Labor, "Workmen's Committees in Czechoslovakia," *Monthly Labor Review* 13 (November 1921): 1147.

46. The Czecho-Slovak Factory Inspection Service was never defined, but it can be reasonably assumed to be a Czechoslovakian government agency that annually inspected the factories.

47. U.S. Department of Labor, "Operation of Works Committees in Czechoslovakia," *Monthly Labor Review* 19 (July 1924): 44.

48. U.S. Department of Labor, "Report on Joint Industrial Councils in England," *Monthly Labor Review* 17 (November 1923): 1017.

49. U.S. Department of Labor, "International Congress on Social Policy at Prague," *Monthly Labor Review* 19 (December 1924): 1386.

50. U.S. Department of Labor, "Establishment of Industrial Councils in the Netherlands," *Monthly Labor Review* 36 (February 1933): 309.

51. Harry Carlson, "Joint Industrial Councils in Great Britain," *Monthly Labor Review* 48 (May 1939): 1046–54.

52. "Joint Production Committees for Royal Ordnance Factories in Great Britain," *International Labour Review* 45 (May 1942): 552–54.

53. "Joint Production Committees," *International Labour Review* 50 (December 1944): 775.

54. "Work Committees in France," *International Labour Review* 50 (September 1944): 364.

55. "Work Committees in France," *International Labour Review* 51 (June 1945): 770–75.

56. Charles Shaw, "Management-Labor Committees," *Industrial and Labor Relations Review* 3 (January 1950): 234.

57. "Joint Committees in Belgium," *International Labour Review* 53 (January 1946): 81.

58. A. Delperee, "Joint Committees in Belgium," *International Labour Review* 81 (March 1960): 191.

59. William McPherson, "Co-determination: Germany's Move Toward a New Economy," *Industrial and Labor Relations Review* 5 (October 1951): 22.

60. Paul Fisher, "Labor Co-determination in Germany," *Social Research* 18 (December 1951): 477.

61. Shaw, op. cit., p. 235.

62. "Establishment of Works Committees in Italy," *International Labour Review* 57 (January 1948): 72–75.

63. "Works Committees in Denmark," *International Labour Review* 57 (April 1948): 365–67.

64. Wilhelm Herschel, "Employee Representation in the Federal Republic of Germany," *International Labour Review* 64 (August–September 1951): 207.

65. Oscar Weigart, "Co-determination in West Germany," *Monthly Labor Review* 73 (December 1951): 651.

66. Clark Kerr, "The Trade Union Movement in the Redistribution of Power in Postwar Germany," *The Quarterly Journal of Economics* 168 (November 1954): 552–53.

67. Theodore Lit, "Expansion of Co-determination in West German Industry," *Monthly Labor Review* 76 (April 1953): 393.

68. Ibid., p. 395.

69. Delperee, op. cit., p. 204.

70. Ibid., p. 185.

71. J.R.P. French, et al., "An Experiment on Participation in a Norwegian Factory," *Human Relations* 13 (1960): 3–19.

72. Ibid., p. 3.

73. Ibid., p. 9.

74. Harriet Holter, "Attitudes Towards Employee Participation in Company Decision Making," *Human Relations* XVIII (1965): 297–321.

75. "Works Committees in France," *International Labour Review* 95 (April 1967): 356.

76. "Workers on the Board," *Time* 105 (May 19, 1975): 57.

3

CO-DETERMINATION IN THE FEDERAL REPUBLIC OF GERMANY

INTRODUCTION

The Federal Republic of Germany was the first nation in the Western world to adopt co-determination and is the nation that has (in 1979) the most far-reaching requirements. Most German companies, including German subsidiaries of U.S. multinationals, are subject to any of four existing co-determination laws. These laws are analyzed in this chapter in three separate sections: Co-determination Laws of 1951 and 1956, Works Constitution Act of 1952, and Co-determination Act of 1976.

CO-DETERMINATION LAWS OF 1951 AND 1956

In the late 1940s, during the occupation after World War II, the British Military Government in Germany approved the German unions' proposal for workers' representation on organizations' boards of directors. The unions wanted to make certain that German industrialists would never again finance a party such as Hitler's, which would again dissolve the trade unions. The German unions' proposal suggested that in companies in the coal, steel, and iron industries, workers' representatives would occupy half of the seats on the companies' supervisory boards. The workers' representatives would be nominated by the company's works councils and appropriate unions combined. A second requirement called for a worker director on the company's board of management.

At the end of the occupation period, the German legislative bodies were not willing to require co-determination by law. "The unions, however, by threatening a general strike, compelled the German legislators in 1951 to enact a special law for the coal, iron and steel industries—in essence, giving legal effect to the system of co-determination already described."[1] This law was called the Co-determination Law (*Mitbestimmungsgesetz*) of 1951.

A graphical overview of the legal requirements of the Co-determination Law of 1951 is presented in Figure 3.1. All companies with more than 1,000 employees in the coal, iron, and steel industries are covered by this law. The structure of a supervisory board with 11 members is analyzed in Figure 3.1. Companies with a capital of 20 million Deutsche Mark (D.M.) (approximately 10 million dollars) must make provisions for a supervisory board of 15 members, and companies with capital of over 50 million D.M. (approximately 25 million dollars) must have a supervisory board of 21 members.

All members of the supervisory board are appointed by the general meeting of stockholders, but there are certain restrictions as to whom the stockholders can appoint. The purpose of these restrictions is to incorporate workers' participation. The following composition is required in the Co-determination Law of 1951 for a supervisory board of 11 members: (1) four stockholders' representatives and a "further member," (2) four employees' representatives and a "further member," and (3) a neutral member.

The general meeting of stockholders can appoint four stockholders' representatives without restrictions and a "further member" with the restrictions that this person (1) must be independent of both employers' and employees' organizations, (2) cannot be an employee of the organization, and (3) must not have a financial interest in the organization. These five supervisory board members are the stockholders' representatives.

The workers' representatives group on the supervisory board also consists of five persons. Two must be workers nominated by the works council. The works council has to discuss its nominations with the appropriate unions which have veto power. The other three are nominated by the unions recognized by the company. These unions can discuss their nominations with the works council, but the latter has no veto power. The "further member," nominated by the unions, is subject to the same restrictions as the stockholders' "further member."[2] These five supervisory board members combined are the workers' representatives. The general meeting of stockholders is obligated to appoint these five workers' representatives to the supervisory board.

The stockholders' and workers' representatives combined nominate the eleventh member. One restriction is that at least three members of the stockholders' representatives must favor the nominated eleventh member.

The Co-determination Law of 1951 also calls for a worker director on the board of management. The primary tasks of the worker director are industrial relations and personnel affairs. No worker director can be appointed by the supervisory board without a majority of the workers' representatives being in favor.[3] This means that the election depends upon the unions' approval.

FIGURE 3.1. Requirements of the German Co-determination Law of 1951.

The general assembly of shareholders elect all members of the supervisory board; at the employees' representatives side they are obligated to appoint the works' council's and the union's nominees.

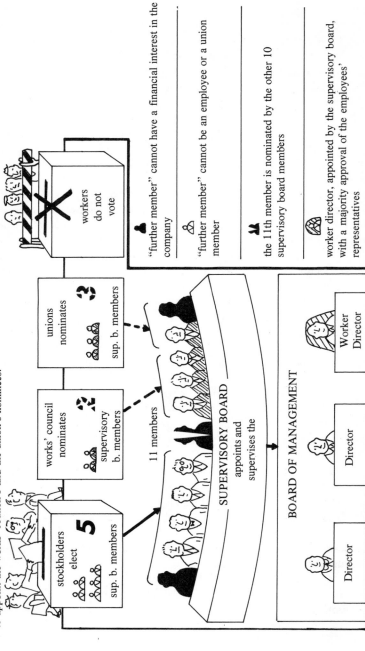

"further member" cannot have a financial interest in the company

"further member" cannot be an employee or a union member

the 11th member is nominated by the other 10 supervisory board members

worker director, appointed by the supervisory board, with a majority approval of the employees' representatives

Source: Roland Tittel, *Mitbestimmung: Forderungen und Tatsachen* (Köln: Deutsches Industreinstitut, 1977) p. 17. Translation from German into English is by the author.

The Co-determination Amendment Law of 1956 resulted only in minor changes and the law affected only three companies. The Co-determinaton Law of 1951 was extended to include those holding companies of which more than half of the revenues came from activities in the coal, iron, and steel industries. The major changes for these companies were that the supervisory board must consist of 15 persons and the worker director must be elected by a majority vote of the total supervisory board.

Representatives of the German iron and steel company Hoesch AG, located in Dortmund, West Germany, were interviewed in September 1975. The purpose was to determine the extent to which co-determination affected managerial decision making and industrial relations at Hoesch.[4] The highlights of these interviews are incorporated in Chapter 8. Only the organizational structure of Hoesch AG is discussed here, as an example of a company subject to the Co-determination Law of 1951.

In 1871, the Hoesch family founded an iron and steel factory. Dortmund as a location site was selected based on the area's large coal reserves and the city's train connections. Significant growth took place and in 1975 Hoesch AG merged with the Dutch company Koninklijke Nederlandsche Hoogovens en Staalfabrieken NV. The two companies now operate under the holding company called ESTEL NV, Hoesch-Hoogovens, registered as a Dutch company. However, each of the two companies has its own supervisory board.

Hoesch AG is subject to the Co-determination Law of 1951, as it employs over 50,000 persons and operates in the iron and steel industries. Figure 3.2. is an overview of the organizational structure and election process of the supervisory board and board of management of Hoesch AG. Subject to earlier outlined legal requirements, the shareholders nominate ten stockholders' representatives, the works councils nominate four workers' representatives, and the unions nominate six workers' representatives. The 20 supervisory board members nominate one additional neutral member. The general meeting of stockholders must appoint all nominated supervisory board members. The six-member Board of Management is appointed by the Supervisory Board. The Board of Management, through its worker director, has to inform the workers of its actions. Figure 3.3. is a self-explanatory overview of the communication and information processes at Hoesch AG.

WORKS CONSTITUTION ACT OF 1952

Co-determination was extended to all other industries in the Works Constitution Act (*Betriebsverfassungsgesetz*) of 1952. Most German public stock companies [*Aktiengesellschaften, (AG)*] and private limited liability companies [*Gesellschaften mit beschränkter Haftung, (GmbH)*] are subject to this law. Exempted are family-owned public stock companies with less than

FIGURE 3.2. Organizational structure and election process of decision-making boards at Hoesch AG.

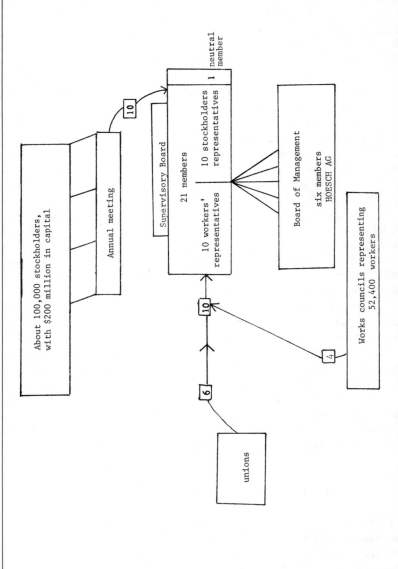

About 100,000 stockholders, with $200 million in capital

Annual meeting

10

Supervisory Board

21 members

10 workers' representatives

10 stockholders representatives

1 neutral member

Board of Management

six members

HOESCH AG

10

Works councils representing 52,400 workers

4

6

unions

Source: Hoesch AG, unpublished overview.

FIGURE 3.3. Information flow at Hoesch AG.

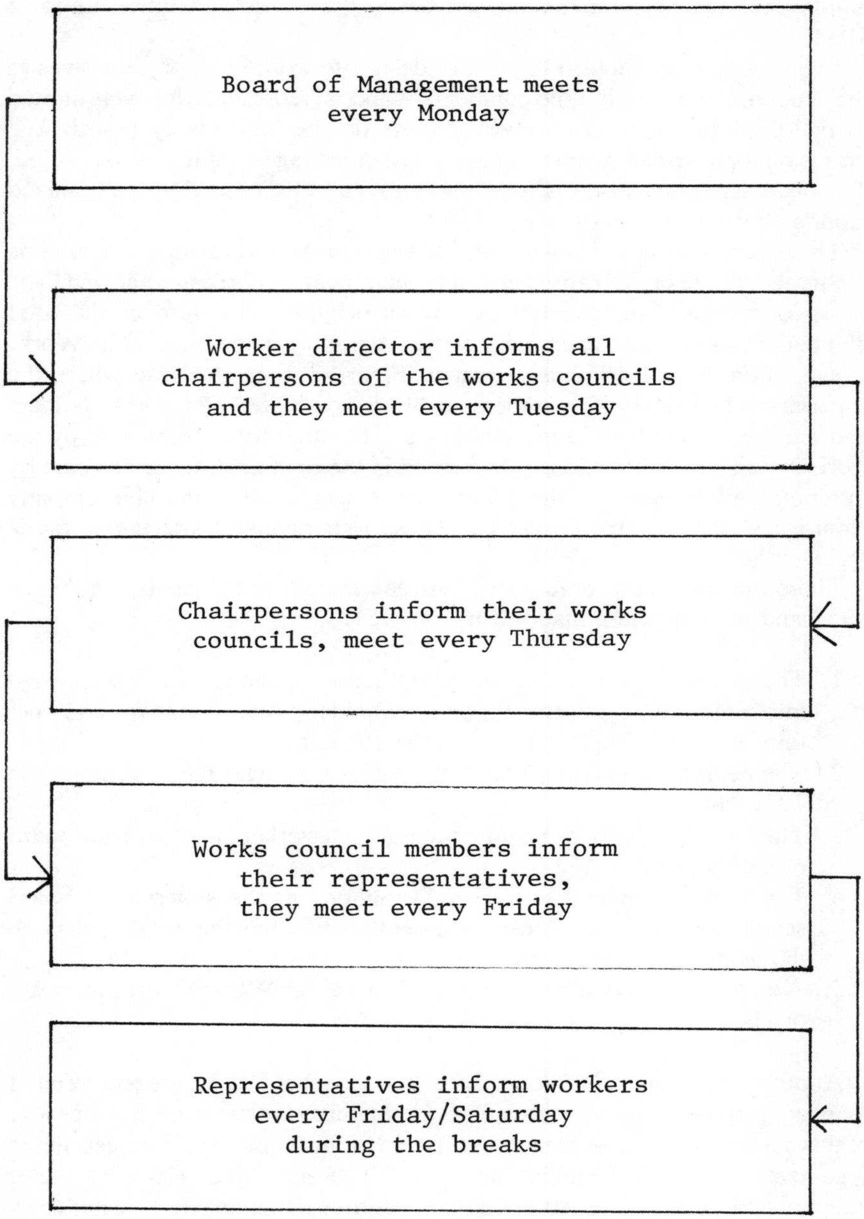

Board of Management meets
every Monday

Worker director informs all
chairpersons of the works councils
and they meet every Tuesday

Chairpersons inform their works
councils, meet every Thursday

Works council members inform
their representatives,
they meet every Friday

Representatives inform workers
every Friday/Saturday
during the breaks

Source: Hoesch AG, unpublished overview.

500 employees, all private limited liability companies with fewer than 500 employees, and those companies subject to the Co-determination Laws of 1951.

Labor was again allowed to elect or designate workers' representatives to the supervisory board, but the number of workers' representatives was limited to one-third of the total number of seats on the supervisory board. The provision for a worker director on the board of management was also omitted. The decrease in the workers' share was a result of a reduction in organized labor's power between 1951 and 1952.

The supervisory board must have between three and 21 members depending on the size of the organization, and only increments of three are allowed. The group of workers' representatives always occupies one-third of the total number of seats on the supervisory board. A graphical overview of the Works Constitution Act of 1952 is shown in Figure 3.4. In the case where the supervisory board has 12 members, eight are nominated by the shareholders and are the stockholders' representatives. The other four, nominated by the works council and the unions represented in the organization, are elected by the company's workers. Of these four members, at least two must be company employees and the others may be. These four members are the workers' representatives.

There are five major differences between the Works Constitution Act of 1952 and the Co-determination Law of 1951:

1. The requirement for parity co-determination in the 1951 law is changed into a requirement of two-thirds stockholders' representatives and one-third workers' representatives in the 1952 law.
2. The neutral supervisory board member is no longer required under the 1952 law.
3. The 1952 law contains no requirement for a worker director on the board of management.
4. The importance and power of the unions in the supervisory board selection process is reduced as under the 1952 law the workers elect all the workers' representatives directly.
5. A larger number of companies are subject to the Works Constitution Act of 1952.

Another provision in the Works Constitution Act of 1952 is the requirement for every private company to create works councils (*Betriebsrat*). The purpose of this act was to increase the representation of the employees' interests in the organization's decision-making processes. The employees elect, by secret ballot, the members of the works council. "Although the right to vote and to be elected to the works council is not dependent on trade union membership, well

FIGURE 3.4. Requirements of the German Works Constitution Act of 1952: Example for a public stock company with 12 supervisory board members.

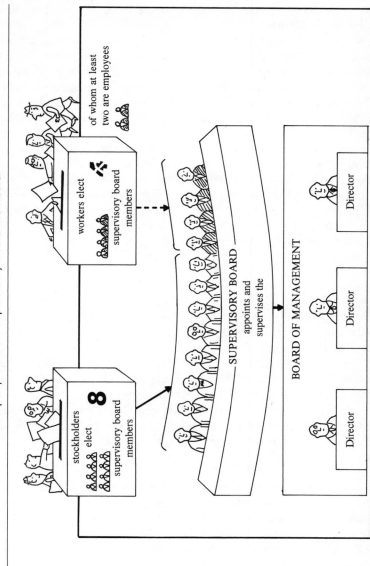

of whom at least two are employees

workers elect supervisory board members

stockholders elect 8 supervisory board members

SUPERVISORY BOARD
appoints and supervises the

BOARD OF MANAGEMENT

Director

Director

Director

Source: Roland Tittel, *Mitbestimmung: Forderungen und Tatsachen* (Köln: Deutsches Industrienstitut, 1977) p. 16. 'Translation from German into English is by the author.

over 80 percent of the members of works councils elected at the last election belong to the trade union."[5]

The works council has the right to participate in social, personnel, financial, and economic matters. Participation in decision making on social matters includes topics such as working hours, vacation arrangements, training, social facilities (such as recreation facilities), and the fixing of piecework and bonus rates. The works council is allowed to participate in personnel matters as well. Topics here include hiring, grouping and regrouping, and mass dismissal of personnel.

The works council can also participate in financial and economic matters. In organizations with more than 20 employees, the works council must approve any organizational changes planned by the employer that may result in a reduction of the employment level for the company as a whole or a large part of the organization. This includes topics such as closure or transfer of production facilities, reduction in the work force, mergers, and introductions of new working and management procedures.[6]

CO-DETERMINATION ACT OF 1976

In February 1974, the West German government proposed a bill to change the co-determination requirements for companies with 2,000 or more employees. The bill was aimed at realizing equal rights and equal weight of the production factors, work, and capital within the decision-making process of companies. The German legislative bodies wished to extend parity co-determination to a larger section of German industries.

On July 1, 1976, the German socialist-liberal coalition government implemented the German Co-determination Act of 1976. This law applies to all joint stock companies and companies with limited liability in Germany except:

1. Companies in the coal, iron, and steel industries (they are still subject to the 1951 co-determination law and its 1956 amendment)
2. Enterprises with less than 2,000 employees (which are covered by the Works Constitution Act of 1952)
3. All political, religious, educational, artistic, and charitable organizations and news media.[7]

The percentage of the total number of supervisory board seats held by workers' representatives increases from 33 to 50 percent.[8] This law affects the 600 largest West German companies. No exceptions are allowed for foreign direct investments in West Germany. This means that more than 30 subsidiaries of U.S. companies, with a combined payroll of close to 200,000 persons, are subject to this co-determination law. Some of these subsidiaries are Deutsche Texaco A.G., Esso A.G., Ford Werke Aktiengesellschaft, Kodak Aktiengesellschaft, Adam Opel Aktiengesellschaft, Avon Cosmetics GmbH, Deutsche Goodyear GmbH, and IBM Deutschland GmbH.[9]

The Co-determination Act of 1976 provides for a regulation of parity co-determination. Therefore, 50 percent of the supervisory board members are elected by the shareholders and the other 50 percent consists of members indirectly elected by the enterprise's employees via a group of electors. The total number of an organization's supervisory board members varies and depends on the number of employees. When the organization has between 2,000 and 10,000 employees, the supervisory board will consist of 12 members. The law requires 16 supervisory board members for an organization with 10,000 to 20,000 employees and 20 supervisory board members for an organization with over 20,000 employees.

An overview of the statutory organizational design of the supervisory and management board levels for an organization with 2,000 to 10,000 employees, satisfying the Co-determination Act of 1976, is presented in Figure 3.5. In this case, the supervisory board is legally required to have 12 members, six representing the shareholders and six employees. The six-member labor representation is composed of four company employees [including at least one blue collar, and one white collar workers' representative and one management employee or senior executive (Leitende Angestellte)], and any additional seats for the company employees are divided in proportion to the number of blue collar and white collar workers and management employees (see Figure 3.5 and Table 3.1). The other two supervisory board members on the labor side represent trade unions active in the company.

The shareholders' representatives are nominated and elected by the general assembly of shareholders. The nomination procedure for employees' representatives is as follows: the trade unions active in the company nominate two or three union leaders as employees' representatives for the supervisory board, and the other employees' representatives are nominated by the company employees. All employees' representatives, whether nominated by the unions or employees, must be elected by the employees.

The next step is the selection of a supervisory board chairman and vice-chairman. The supervisory board members elect these two people from among themselves. A two-thirds majority is required for election, and a second election is called for when such a majority does not materialize. The stockholders' representatives, in this case, elect the supervisory board chairman and the employees' representatives elect the vice-chairman. A simple majority of votes is then sufficient.

The importance of the chairman is signified by the fact that he has the power to break a tie vote. With only a few exceptions, all decisions of the supervisory board are made with a simple majority vote. In the case of a deadlock situation

FIGURE 3.5. Overview of the statutory organizational design of the supervisory and management board level for an organization satisfying the German Co-determination Act of 1976.

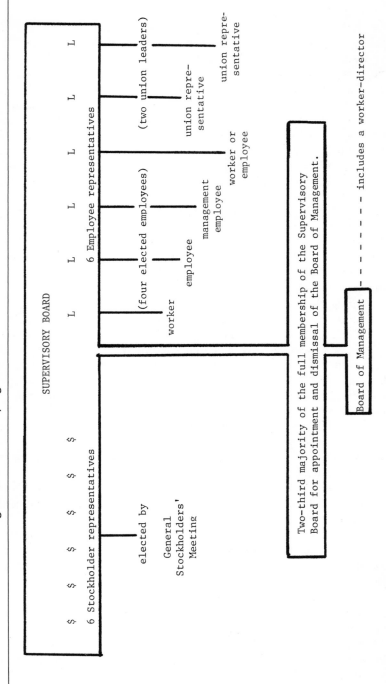

Source: Constructed by the author.

TABLE 3.1. Graphical overview of the number and type of representatives on the supervisory board level, based on the German Co-determination Act of 1976.

Total number of employees	Total Number of Supervisory Board Members	Total Number of Stockholders' Representatives	Employees' representatives	
			Union Representatives	Company Employees*
2,000 to 10,000	12	6	2	4
10,001 to 20,000	16	8	2	6
over 20,000	20	10	3	7

*This group of employee representatives must be employed by the company and the group must include at least one blue collar, as well as, one white collar workers' representative and one management employees' representative.

Source: Compiled by the author.

a second vote can be called for. If a deadlock occurs again, then the chairman has the tie-breaking vote by the fact that his vote will count double.

The supervisory board appoints the board of management. Two-thirds of the supervisory board must be in favor of the proposed board of management. If this majority is not reached, then "an arbitration committee of two shareholders and two labor representatives will seek to propose a candidate in the second round of voting, where a simple majority will suffice for installment."[10] If a need exists for a third election then, again, the supervisory board's chairman has a tie-breaking vote.

A further special provision concerns the appointment of a worker director to the board of management. This requirement was also included in the Co-determination Law of 1951. The worker director has equal voting rights to any other board of management member and is in most cases a personnel director.

CONCLUSION

Co-determination requirements in the Federal Republic of West Germany are rather complex and sometimes even confusing. All companies in the coal, iron, and steel industries with over 1,000 employees are subject to the Co-determination Law of 1951. All other companies with 500 to 2,000 employees are subject to the Works Constitution Act of 1952. Companies employing over

2,000 employees outside the coal, iron, and steel industries must adhere to the Co-determination Act of 1976.

No exceptions have been made in the German co-determination legislation for foreign direct investments. the larger subsidiaries of U.S. multinationals are, therefore, subject to co-determination requirements.

NOTES

1. Wolfgang Heintzeler, "Is the American Board of the 1980's Now Being Tested in Europe?," Paper presented at the Corporate Directors' Conference, Washington, D.C., December 17, 1974, p. 4.

2. See: Horst-Udo Niedenhoff, *Mitbestimmung im Betrieb und Unternehmen* (Köln: Deutscher Instituts-Verlag GmbH, 1973), p. 23.

3. Arbeitskreises Mitbestimmung, *Stellungnahme des Arbeitskreises Mitbestimmung zum Mitbestimmungsgesetz* (Köln: Bundesvereinigung der Deutschen Arbeitgeberverbände 1976), p. 17.

4. The author expresses sincere thanks for their cooperation to those managers and employees of Hoesch AG who participated in the interviews.

5. Commission of the European Communities, *Employee Participation and Company Structure* (Brussels: EEC, 1975), p. 59.

6. Walter Stolz, "How the Workers Participate in German Industry," *The Director*, 27 (September 1974): 348; Tittel, op. cit., pp. 10–11; Commission of the European Communities, op. cit., p. 60.

7. German Information Center, "Co-determination, A Survey of the Bill on Employee Participation in Management Decision Making," unpublished paper, October 1964, p. 3.

8. Several sources are available describing the legal requirements of the Co-determination Act of 1976. Some of the sources used for the description included here are: German Information Center, *op. cit.*, pp. 4–5; Institut der Deutschen Wirtschaft, "Argumente zu Unternehmerfragen," No. 2, 1976; Informationsdienst des Instituts der Deutschen Wirtschaft, "Der Entwurf des neuen Mitbestimmungsgesetzes," IWD newsletter, Jahrgang 2, No. 12, March 18, 1976, pp. 4–6; "Mitbestimmung: Gut für die Koalition," *Der Spiegel* (1975): 25–26; Heinz Hartman, *Ibid.*, p. 59; Confederation of German Employers' Associations, "Comments of the Confederation of German Employers' Associations on the Government Projects in the Field of Parity Co-determination and Asset Formation," unpublished paper, May 17, 1974; Friedrich Fürstenburg, "West German Experience with Industrial Democracy," *The Annals* 431 (May 1977): 32–43.

9. Hans Bockler Gesellschaft eV, "Das Mitbestimmungsgespräch," *Gewerkschaftliche Monatshefte* (October, November, December, 1973): 216–22.

10. German Information Service, op. cit., p. 5.

4

INDUSTRIAL DEMOCRACY
IN THE BENELUX COUNTRIES
AND SCANDINAVIA

Several hundred U.S. companies have investments in the Benelux countries. Therefore, they keep close track of the co-determination developments in this region. The purpose of the earlier part of this chapter is to analyze the industrial democracy requirements in the Netherlands, Belgium, and Luxembourg. The Netherlands has a unique form of co-determination; works councils are the only requirement in Belgium; Luxembourg has limited co-determination requirements.

The Scandinavian countries are often considered leaders in industrial democracy. An analysis of the contemporary industrial relations requirements in Norway, Denmark, and Sweden is included in the latter part of this chapter.

THE NETHERLANDS

In July 1973, new corporate legislation was put into effect in the Netherlands.[1] This legislation included requirements for employee councils and a unique form of co-determination. Three main motives were behind this new corporate legislation: (1) to increase the visibility of the corporation's financial situation to its shareholders, employees, and third parties involved in trade with the corporation; (2) to increase workers' participation; and (3) to increase the supervision of the organization's day-to-day operations.

Employee Councils

The functions and organization of the works councils (*ondernemingsraden*) in the Netherlands were extended in 1973 through an amendment of the original 1950 legislation on works councils. Management is now required to provide the organization's works councils with information about the organization, and the works councils have the right to participate in decisions in matters of social nature such as working conditions, vacations, and participation in profits.

All public and closed companies with over 100 employees must organize one or more works councils. A "central works council" must be set up if more than one works council exists and a majority of the councils so request. Group or division works councils may be organized as an intermediate level between the works councils and the central works council. This means that councils can be placed together in "group works councils" based on specific activities of a group.

In the case of N.V. Philips in the Netherlands, 78 percent of all Philips employees in that country executed their voting right in April 1975 to elect approximately 1,400 persons to 116 works councils. These 116 works councils are again organized into 24 group councils, representing employees in divisions such as glass, light, and video. Representatives of the 24 group works councils at Philips occupy 32 seats on the central works council.

The law requires that a member of the company's board of management be chairman of the central works council. This requirement resulted in criticism from most Dutch unions. Since early 1976, the labor government of the Netherlands, acting under pressure from the labor unions, is considering eliminating this requirement.

In February 1976, *Elsevier Magazine* published the results of an opinion poll. The Dutch labor government was not content with the opinion poll outcome and tried to cover up the results.[2] The objective of the opinion poll was to measure (1) whether or not the works council law, as implemented in June 1973, should be changed, and (2) whether or not a member of the board of management should be chairman of the central works council. The results of the January 16, 1976 opinion poll revealed that (1) only 26 percent of the Dutch population sample wanted an urgent change in the works councils legislation, and (2) 65 percent of the employees approved the fact that a member of the board of management occupies the central works council's chairman position.

Co-determination and the Corporate Law of 1973

Three major changes in the organizational structure were the result of the Corporate Law of 1973. This law applies to all organizations with a capital, including reserves of at least 4 million dollars, and 100 or more employees:

1. The organization is required to have a supervisory board.
2. The members of the board of management are appointed by the

supervisory board, and the board of management is responsible for the day-to-day operations of the organization.

3. New supervisory board members are to be appointed by the present members of the supervisory board.

Several characteristics and implications of the election process are:[3]

1. Members of the supervisory board get appointed for four renewable terms.
2. The supervisory board members are no longer appointed or reappointed by the annual meeting of shareholders; these members are appointed by the present supervisory board members. This requirement may result in a reduction of the shareholders' control over their organization.
3. Both shareholders and the central works council can propose prospective supervisory board members, but the final choice remains with the supervisory board itself.
4. Both the central works council and annual meeting of shareholders have the right to veto a supervisory board appointment.
5. The supervisory board can try to revoke this veto by appealing to the national Social-Economic Council (SER), which can override a veto.
6. The annual meeting of shareholders is permitted to appoint a shareholders' committee to represent and protect their interests.

The purpose of this organizational structure (see Figure 4.1.) is to create a supervisory board based on the confidence of both shareholders and employees and geared toward the interests of the organization as a whole. In comparison, workers do not have a block of representatives on the supervisory board as in West Germany; however, their approval along with that of the shareholders is needed for any board nominee. Finally, it should be noted that trade union officials and employees of the organization cannot obtain seats on the supervisory board. It is hoped that this structure will avoid the West German system's problem of stalemates when representatives of the shareholders and employees vote as opposing blocks.

The following exceptions to these legal requirements exist for multinationals operating in the Netherlands. Any company with more than 50 percent of its workers employed outside the Dutch boundries is only subject to the law with respect to its operations within the Netherlands. The multinational must create a subsidiary in the Netherlands with a supervisory board and a board of management (assuming that the subsidiary has more than 100 employees). The election of the supervisory board members is handled in the manner explained above. An exception here is that the board of management is not appointed by the supervisory board, but by the annual meeting of stockholders (that is, the international mother company).

FIGURE 4.1. Structure of a Dutch organization.

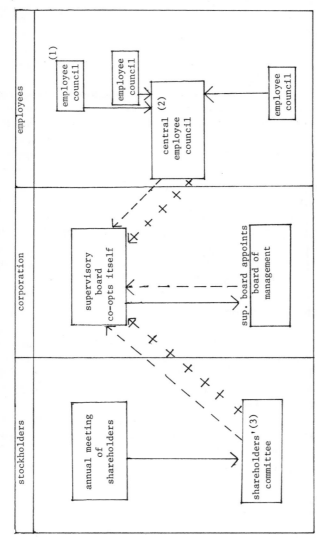

--→ direction of recommendations on a prospective supervisory board member.
xxxx direction of possible veto on a prospective supervisory board member.
(1) employees of division or enterprise elect the employee council.
(2) when there is no central employees' council, then the individual employee councils execute the right to recommend and the veto right.
(3) when there is no shareholders' committee, then the annual meeting of shareholders executes the right to recommend and the veto right.

Source: T. Drion, "De herbouw van ons ondernemingsrecht," *Op Eigen Terrein* (March 16, 1972): 9. Translation from Dutch into English is by the author.

In summary, the Netherlands has an unusual provision whereby the workers cannot be on the supervisory board or have a direct say in the appointment of its members. The latter elects its own members, but both the annual meeting of shareholders and the central works council have veto power over all proposed future members of the supervisory board. In some cases, as successfully done by Akzo-Nederland B.V., the supervisory board invites the works council to propose a board member. If no final decision can be reached, the case is decided by the Social-Economic Council.

The major point of the co-determination system in the Netherlands is that no direct workers' participation takes place. Employees have an indirect voice in decisions concerning future supervisory board members through their veto power. The purpose of this system is to create a harmonious supervisory board geared toward the interests of the organization at large and not a single interest group.[4]

BELGIUM

There is no provision for workers' participation on the decision-making boards of companies in the private sector in Belgium.[5] At present, all enterprises employing 150 or more persons must set up works councils. The head of the corporation is the chairman of the works council. Belgian unions are pushing the government to abolish this last requirement and to extend the power of the works council to include a veto right in decisions related to changes in work rules, layoffs, closures, and investments.

The administrative structure of the Belgian private corporations includes the commissioners (*commissaires*), who are responsible for the supervision of the company's financial and legal operations, which are executed by a council of administration (*conseil d'administration*) of at least three persons. Both the commissioners and the members of the council of administration are hired and fired by the general assembly of shareholders. In reality, the council of administration often appoints an executive committee responsible for the day-to-day operations. The council of administration limits itself, then, to a supervisory capacity.

To end this confusing administrative structure, the Belgian government is currently studying the possibilities of requiring a supervisory board and a board of management as used in many other European countries. There is no real union pressure for extending workers' participation to the decision-making bodies of corporations.

LUXEMBOURG

The administrative structure of companies in Luxembourg is similar to that of Belgium, with commissioners, a council of administration, and an executive committee. A unique feature is the personnel council, which is required in every company with 150 or more employees. It is a mixed committee composed equally of employer and employee representatives. The personnel council's employee representatives are composed of both a delegation representing blue collar workers and a delegation representing white collar workers, whereby the size of these two delegations varies with the proportional basis of the number of employees in each group.

It is required by law that the council of administration (*conseil d'administration*) in companies with 1,000 or more employees consists of one-third workers' representatives, designated by the personnel council and chosen from among the company's employees. (The Arbed Steel company is the only corporation in Luxembourg with more than 1,000 employees.) The unions demand 50 percent of the council's seats for workers.

NORWAY

The oil and gas developments on the North Sea will probably put Norway among the world's wealthiest nations in a few years.[6] The expected inflow of funds will have a significant impact upon the economic development of Norway, and the per capita income can be expected to rise over the next years. Whether this increase in per capita income will alter labor's attitude toward co-determination is yet to be seen. In 1974, Tor Aspengren, the president of the Norwegian Trade Union Federation, expressed labor's opinion:

> Democracy in industry is dependent upon a broad co-influence by workers. What we usually conceive by the term co-influence is that employees in different ways have a real possibility of influencing the various conditions at the work place.... What is decisive in the first place, however, is the general climate for human contact and the existence of mutual understanding and respect. In a democratic industrial setting the views of the employees will influence the life of the undertaking even if they do not have the formal right of co-determination.

The desire among unions for a more harmonious relationship between management and labor is in line with the government's decision not to render the control of workers' participation to the unions, but to leave it with the workers themselves.

Co-determination was introduced in Norway by law in January 1973. In companies employing more than 200 persons the concept of corporate assembly—analogous to the supervisory boards of West German companies—was introduced. The corporate assembly consists of at least 12 members, of whom one-third are elected by and from among the employees and the remaining two-thirds by stockholders. As in the West German co-determination system, the corporate assembly appoints the board of management. Noticeably different from the German system is the possibility for Norwegian employees' representatives on the corporate assembly to designate directly two members to the board of management. This arrangement introduces workers' participation at the board of management level.

Future changes in the above requirements are expected, as the Norwegian government and unions wish to secure a voice for local municipalities on the boards. This would quite likely have the effect of reducing the employers' representation to 50 percent or less.

DENMARK

In the Company Act of 1973, Denmark followed other European nations by giving workers in firms with 50 or more employees the right to elect at least two employees' representatives for two-year terms to the supervisory board (in Danish: *bestyrelse*).[8] As in Norway, the workers may, but do not have the duty to, elect employees' representatives. A simple majority of the employees must be in favor of the employee representation. As in most other systems, the board of management is appointed by the supervisory board. No substantial proposals are being made to change the present situation.

SWEDEN

Sweden, where labor receives the highest wages in Europe, a paid five-week vacation, and where 90 percent of the blue collar workers are organized, although there is no closed shop, faced in June 1977 its first major strike since 1945.[9] Swedish industry is no longer competitive and has lost shares in the export markets, partly as a result of the high cost of labor. All the individual trade unions, to which 90 percent of the workers belong, are part of the Confederation of Trade Unions (LO). About half of the white collar workers belong to unions that make up the Central Organization of Salaried Employees (TCO).[10] The employers are organized in the Swedish Employers Association (SAF).

In the fall of 1976, a new coalition of Central, Liberal, and Conservative parties headed by the new Prime Minister Thorbjorn Falldin defeated the Social Democratic Party. Falldin removed the restraining influence over labor as well as management that the Social Democrats had exercised during 44 years of power. The Social Democrats had permitted a macro-collective bargaining between the SAF and the LO. The individual trade unions and employer organizations had no power and were under the complete control of the respective national organizations.

If the various national unions and employer associations have comparatively little to say, the individual employee or employer has none. The spirit and the letter of the Swedish collective bargaining legislation favors the organization rather than the individual.[11]

The smaller employer in Sweden has difficulties in keeping up with the high wage demands. The union's policy has not only been the equalization of wages, but also the elimination of smaller firms.[12]

Co-determination has been required by law in Sweden since 1973 for companies with over 100 employees. This law required that two employees' representatives be admitted to the company's board of directors. These representatives, however, have no voting rights in the enterprise's relations with trade unions. The 1976 Act of Employees' Participation in decision making vested all participation rights in the labor unions and no longer in employees. Noteworthy is the fact that the two workers' representatives should be considered the absolute minimum level of participation, and their number can be increased through bargaining agreements.

Swedish unions are actively involved in training workers for board positions. Allamanna Svenska Elektriska AB (ASEA) started an educational program in 1971 designed to give representatives a basic understanding of the economic, production, and personnel factors governing the administration of the company[13]

In summary, as a result of the 44-year leadership of the Social Democrats, Swedish unions have created a powerful position for themselves in the daily economic life of that country. Since 1976, all participation rights have been vested in the labor unions, and no longer with the workers. Changes in the industrial democracy requirements are to be expected from the new government, but it is still too early to draw conclusions.

CONCLUSION

Each of the Benelux and Scandinavian countries has some form of workers' participation. However, each country has one or more unique features which distinguishes it from the others.

In the Netherlands, workers, through their works councils, have a veto right over any proposed supervisory board member. Belgian workers do not participate at the board of directors' level, but they have a voice through their works councils. In Luxembourg, employees occupy 50 percent of the seats of the personnel council. The employer occupies the other seats.

In Norway, workers' representatives on the supervisory board directly appoint two members of the company's board of management. Norway is, therefore, the first country to introduce workers' participation at both the supervisory board and board of management levels. Danish workers have two representatives on the supervisory board. The Swedish LO demanded many social benefits for its workers during the last decades. Among those is the requirement that at least two workers' representatives be admitted on a single board of directors.

In this chapter, the industrial democracy requirements in the Benelux countries and Scandinavia were outlined. These requirements have impact upon the operations of several hundred U.S. companies with investments in these areas.

NOTES

1. The majority of information in this section is based on the author's interviews with Mr. Haighton of Philips N.V. (Eindhoven, The Netherlands), Professor Ivo A.C. van Haren, member of the Supervisory Board of AKZO Nederland B.V. (Velp, The Netherlands), Mr. Nagenius of Nederlandse Unilever-bedrijven B.V. (Rotterdam, The Netherlands), Mr. R. Hoorens van Heijningen and Mr. Vermeulen, both staff member of the Dutch Employers Federation, Verbond van Nederlandse Ondernemingen, VNO (The Hague, The Netherlands). All interviews took place in August 1975 in The Netherlands. The author wishes to express his sincere appreciation to the above gentlemen and organizations for their help.

2. "De verzwegen Nipo-enquete," *Elsevier Magazine* (February 7, 1976):14–15.

3. See: T. Drion, "De herbouw van ons ondernemingsrecht," *Op Eigen Terrein* publication of Unilever N.V., Rotterdam (March 2, March 16 and April 13, 1972).

4. See also: Dr. Ivo A.C. van Haren, *Naar een nieuwe ondernemingsstructuur* (Assen, The Netherlands: Van Gorcum, N.V., 1976); Wiardi Beckman Stichting, *Op weg naar arbeiderszelfbestuur* (Deventer, The Netherlands: Kluwer, 1974).

5. Sources used for the Belgian section include: Commission of the European Communities, *Employee Participation and Company Structure* (Brussels: European Communities Commission, 1975), pp. 49–52; "When Workers Call the Tune in Management," *U.S. News and World Report* (May 10, 1976): 83.

6. Sources used for the Norway section include: Tor Aspengren, "Norway," in *Industry's Democratic Revolution*, ed. Charles Levinson (London: Allen and Urwin, 1974), pp. 219–30; E. Thorsrud and F. Emery, "Industrial Democracy in Norway," *Industrial Relations* 9 (February 1970):187–96; Sam Zagoris, "Policy Implications and Future Agenda," in *The Worker and the Job*, ed. The American Assembly (Englewood Cliffs, N.J.: Prentice Hall, 1974), p. 189; "Workers on the Board," *The Economist* 246 (March 24, 1973):67.

7. Tor Aspengren, op. cit., p. 220.

8. Sources used for the Denmark section include: "Workers on the Board" *The Economist* 246 (March 24, 1973):67; Edmund Fawcett, "European Companies," *European Community*, (July–August 1975):3–4; Prospero, "Inside Europe," *The Director*, 25 (February 1973):172.

9. Sources for the Sweden section include (among others): Bowen Northrup, "Battling Boredom," *The Wall Street Journal* (March 1, 1977):1, 36; Birger Viklund, "Education for Industrial Democracy," *Working Life in Sweden*, ed. Swedish Information Service (New York: Swedish Consulate General, May 1977), pp. 1–4; "When Workers Call the Tune in Management," *U.S. News and World Report*, 80 (May 10, 1976):85–88; *The Economist* (March 24, 1973):67; Ruth Link, "Shop-floor to Top-floor," *Sweden Now* 10 (1976):18–48; 20; Arne Geijer, "Sweden," *Industrial Democratic Revolution*, ed. Charles Levinson (London: Allen and Urwin, 1974), pp. 268–79.

10. Nancy Foy and Herman Gadon, "Worker Participation: Contrasts in Three Countries," *Harvard Business Review* 54 (May–June 1976):73.

11. Alfred L. Thimm, "Recent Trends in German Co-determination Legislation and the Future of Capitalism in Europe," *Administrative and Engineering System Monograph, aes-7701* (January 1977) (Union College and University, Schenectady, New York), p. 6.

12. Ibid., p. 6.

13. Iaon Carson, "Preparing Workers for Participation," *International Management* 28 (January 1973):44–45.

5

OTHER WEST EUROPEAN CO-DETERMINATION REQUIREMENTS AND PROPOSALS

Co-determination is not restricted to the Federal Republic of Germany, the Benelux countries, and Scandinavia. The United Kingdom, France, and the European Economic Community (EEC) are currently considering co-determination proposals. This chapter includes an analysis of these proposals and an overview of the existing co-determination requirements in these areas as well as Austria, Ireland, and Italy.

UNITED KINGDOM

Shock waves went through the United Kingdom's managerial levels when, in February 1977, the Bullock Committee suggested legislation giving labor a larger share of the seats on a corporation's board of directors. In April 1978, this proposal was still in the discussion stage. Attempts to establish legal co-determination requirements are supported by the British federation of trade unions—the Trade Union Congress (TUC).[1] The relationship between labor and management in the United Kingdom is based upon a long history of cooperation and confrontation. Therefore, the analysis of the Bullock report and its implications are preceded by the history of workers' participation in the United Kingdom.

Workers' Participation in the United Kingdom

In the United Kingdom, collective bargaining and joint consultation are historically the processes for workers' participation in management. The union–management negotiations through collective bargaining include topics such as working conditions and reward systems. Discussions concerning the organization's investment and reorganization are excluded from the collective bargaining processes. Some participation in the decision-making processes at the shopfloor level appeared as a result of the Whitley Committee studies during World War I. Workers are allowed to participate in decisions of matters which are not included in the collective bargaining processes but do affect the workers' immediate work environment. This form of participation is often referred to as joint consultation.

In the mid-1960s, the British government established, under pressure from the trade unions, the co-determination concept in nationalized industries. Organized labor won trade union appointments to the managing board, and the British Steel Corporation's attempts to incorporate "worker directors" is an example of this trend.[2]

In May 1968, the nationalized British Steel Corporation, at that time the world's third largest steel producer, incorporated worker directors on the company's decision-making and policy-formulating levels. Twelve workers—including a scrapyard foreman, a blast furnace man, a bricklayer, and a tool room fitter—became part-time directors of one of the four group boards of the British Steel Corporation. These worker directors, which were "hand-picked" by the unions from among the workers, had full voting rights. The worker directors' power was somewhat limited because the four group boards are subordinate to the corporation's main board, which had no worker directors. However, most of the decisions that affect British Steel's employees are made by the four group boards.

Within four years, it was reported that the British Steel Corporation's worker director plan had failed. A research team, appointed at the request of the British Steel Corporation, concluded that the worker director plan was a disappointing experiment. Several reasons were cited for the failure:

1. The worker directors were accused of losing touch with their fellow workers and were, therefore, distrusted by their own colleagues in the steel works and in the steel unions.
2. The worker directors were "hand-picked" by the unions and regarded by the men on the floor as unrepresentative of the average worker.
3. The law denied a normal relationship between the worker directors and their unions, resulting in a situation that the unions ignored the worker directors and behaved as if they did not exist.
4. Management treated the worker directors very much as "second class" management; senior management kept them off the major policy-making committees and frequently denied them access to relevant information, especially on financial matters.[3]

Similar types of complaints were voiced related to the German co-determination system by unions and employer federations in Germany.

The British multinational Imperial Chemical Industries (ICI) designed a policy in the early 1970s to involve employees increasingly in decisions affecting their work and to bring about a change of attitudes between management and employees from the authoritarian, negative approach to a participative problem-solving style. Attempts were made to develop a common identity or interest and involvement between the shopfloor and management.[4] ICI initiated communication and participation systems to develop a better understanding between management and the shopfloor. Informal consultative systems based on local need were organized for ICI's weekly staff (blue collar workers) and monthly staff (white collar workers). The informal consultation was aimed toward enhancing the understanding of the common interests by jointly studying and discussing problems of concern to both management and workers. This means that it involved seeking mutually acceptable solutions through an exchange of views and information.

Committees to discuss business information were created at the local, division, and central or national levels. An exchange of information existed between these committees and the unions respectively at the local, division, and national levels.

The law in the United Kingdom neither requires nor prohibits co-determination, but British employers should expect an increase in demands for co-determination. Three major political parties in England included discussions about co-determination in their political programs for the 1975 elections. This resulted in the appointment in 1975 of a special study committee, chaired by Oxford historian Lord Bullock. In early February 1977, this committee presented a proposal, commonly known as the Bullock Report.

The Bullock Report

The main recommendation in the Bullock Report is to suggest legislation requiring corporations in the private sector to accept workers' representatives on the board of directors. The Bullock committee suggests giving labor and stockholders an identical number of seats on the board of directors and a smaller number of seats to impartial outsiders. The third group of directors, the outsiders, (1) must occupy less than one-third of all the board of directors' seats, (2) may not represent any distinct interest group, and (3) must be of an odd number. These outsiders are appointed by agreement between the stockholders' representatives and the workers' representatives on the board of directors. When these parties cannot come to an agreement, then the Industrial Democracy Commission will make a choice.

All corporations in the private sector with 2,000 or more employees will be subject to these requirements when this Bullock proposal becomes law. However, a corporation is not required to implement this workers' participation requirement if the proposal does not carry the support of the corporation's workers. If at least one-third of all eligible workers vote in favor of board representation, then the realignment of the board begins.[5] It is estimated that the law would apply to more than 700 companies, including the subsidiaries of over 100 foreign multinational corporations.

The Institute of Directors and the Confederation of British Industries oppose the proposals as outlined in the Bulllock Report, and these organizations threatened to discontinue any cooperation with the labor government.[6] Positive remarks about the Bullock Report were voiced by the Trade Union Congress, and they will push for legal adoption of the proposal by the British Parliament.

The future of the Bullock Report is not yet clear. The unions and labor government are in favor of the proposals, but they meet strong opposition from managers and owners of equity, including those from the United States.

German Co-determination versus the Bullock Report

Since July 1976, the German law provides employee representatives with 50 percent of the seats on the supervisory board. Major differences between this German co-determination model and the Bullock Report are:

1. An "outsiders" group of directors is not incorporated in the German system, where only representatives of the employees and stockholders are on the supervisory board.
2. The German co-determination law does not go as far as the Bullock proposal in reducing the shareholders' control. In Germany, stockholders lose 50 percent of their ownership, but under the Bullock proposal over 50 percent.
3. The German law requires a two-tier board of directors—the supervisory board and the board of management. The British law requires a one-tier board of directors.

In Germany, co-determination takes place on the supervisory board, which means that the employee representatives do not participate in the day-to-day operations. The British plan is to put the original management in a minority position on the management board itself, giving workers and outsiders power to run the business.

THE EUROPEAN ECONOMIC COMMUNITY

The development of each of the nine Member States of the EEC, referred to as the "Nine" or the "Member States," must be seen within the context of the historical, economic, and social conditions of the country concerned.[7] At present, substantial differences among the Nine exist based on these various historical, economic, and social conditions. The Commission of the European Communities feels that a failure to construct a common social foundation may result in the collapse of the EEC.

> There is a serious danger that, sooner or later, the needs and interests of certain parts of the Community will be so different from those of other parts, that the existing Community arrangements will be insufficient to take the strain. Similarly, only by developing a common structural foundation can the Member States hope to adopt more united policies as to the world outside.[8]

Several attempts were made by the commission to close the gap between each Member State's national laws pertaining to joint-stock companies. Corporations operating in two or more EEC countries are subject to different laws containing various requirements for the internal structure of companies, the power of directors, and the rights of shareholders and employees.

The European Company Statute

A campaign to align the company laws of the EEC Member States resulted in the original proposal for a Statute for the European Company in June 1970. To explain certain details of this proposal, the EEC commission published its thoughts about a European Company Statute.

The European Commission's proposal would encourage transnational business and workers' participation. The proposal offers companies (U.S. subsidiaries included) doing business in more than one Member State the option of registering as a "European Company" (*Société Européenne*, SE) instead of registering under existing national laws. The European Company Statute would be optional and no enterprise would be compelled to use this framework. They could choose to do so by fulfilling the requirements of the statute, including a provision for co-determination.[9]

An international business operating in the EEC is subject to nine different legal systems. Branches of foreign enterprises are often looked upon with suspicion and may be treated that way by the host country. Setting up separate subsidiaries in each of the nine Member States can result in organizational structures not suitable for an enterprise that wishes to operate in the community as freely as in its own home country. To register as a European Company will result in "the assurances of freedom from frequent and often unpredictable changes in national law that can scramble well-laid investment plans."[10]

A second feature of the European Company Statute will be that it facilitates the restructuring of corporations within the EEC on an international basis. The statute will enable mergers to take place in a much more rational way than in the past, as many of the legal complexities will have been removed. Up to now, different legal requirements in each of the Nine made mergers across national frontiers almost impossible. Only through complex structures, such as in the case of the merger between the German Hoesch A.G. and the Dutch Koninklijke Nederlandsche Hoogovens en Staalfabrieken N.V. into Estel N.V., is a rational reorganization of the legal structures of corporations across national boundries possible.

European Economic Community's Workers' Participation

The European Company Statute also includes a provision for co-determination. Organizations that would choose to implement the new European Company Statute must obtain a specific board of directors level structure, with obligations in relation to shareholders, creditors, employees, and society as a whole. The organization will be required to have a two-tier management system, which will divide the supervisory and management functions respectively between the supervisory board and the board of executive directors or board of management, rather than a single board of directors. The supervisory board will appoint, fire, and supervise the board of management and its activities. The board will be responsible for the organization's day-to-day operations. Employees' participation will take place at the supervisory board level.

The composition of the supervisory board will be based on a three-way split: one-third representatives of shareholders, one-third employees' representatives, and one-third "independents." The members of the troika will equally share all strategic decision making. The "independents" can be neither shareholders nor employees and must represent "general interest," which incorporates the feature of enabling other broader interests than those of the shareholders and employees to be represented on the supervisory board.

All employees in a particular country who work for a European Company or one of its subsidiaries elect members for national works councils. The trade unions represented in the company propose candidates for workers' representatives on the supervisory board. However, the members of the national works councils elect the workers' representatives from among the proposed candidates.

The election process of supervisory board members consists of two steps: (1) the shareholders elect their representatives and the national works councils elect the employees' representatives, and (2) the independents or general interests' representatives are appointed by agreement of the shareholders' representatives and the employees' representatives on the supervisory board, with a two-thirds majority vote. A graphical overview of the supervisory board's composition and the two-step election process is provided in Figure 5.1. The total number of supervisory board members must be uneven to prevent deadlock situations during voting.

All corporations with 500 or more employees and operating in the private sector which have decided to become European Companies would be subject to these requirements. Corporations are not required to implement co-determination if the proposal does not carry the support of the corporation's workers. When a majority of the workers vote in favor of board representation, then the realignment of the board begins. If the employees reject co-determination, the corporation can become a European Company all the same.

United Kingdom and West Germany versus European Economic Community Workers' Participation

The main recommendation of the British labor government in the Bullock Report is to propose legislation requiring corporations in the private sector to accept workers' participation on the board of directors. The proposal in the Bullock Report is akin to the European Company Statute, as the Bullock committee suggests giving labor and stockholders an identical number of seats on the board of directors and a smaller number of seats to "impartial outsiders."

There are two major differences between the West German Co-determination Law of 1976 and the European Company Statute: (1) a "general interest" group of directors is not incorporated in the German system; only stockholders' and employees' representatives are on the supervisory board, (2) the German co-determination law does not go as far as the statute in reducing the shareholders' control. The European Commission does not agree to this second point. Their spokesman stated that "the Commission would never go as far as the German parity co-determination, nor would their proposal be as rigorous."[11] The German law reduces the number of seats occupied by shareholders' representatives to 50 percent and leaves the tie-breaking vote in the hands of shareholders' representatives. The EEC plans to reduce the number of seats occupied by shareholders' representatives by two-thirds. The degree to which share holders will lose control over their investment fully depends on the cooperation between the shareholders' representatives and the general interests' representatives, whereby it must be added that the latter are elected by both the shareholders' representatives and the employees' representatives.

FIGURE 5.1. Design of the supervisory and management board structure of an organization subject to the European Company Statute.

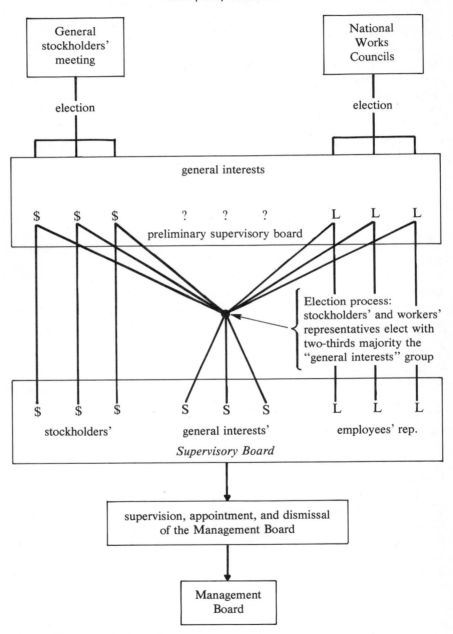

Source: Constructed by the author.

The Future of the European Company Statute

Multinational corporations may wish to register as a European Company for its legal simplicity, its uniform interpretation of the European court, and its stable legal regime. At the same time, they will face a variety of constraints and a drastic reduction of headquarters' control and influence over the decision-making processes and formulation of corporate policies and strategies. It is safe to assume that the general interests' representatives will play an important part in the decision-making processes. When the representatives of employees and shareholders have conflicting ideas, it is up to the general interests' representatives to cast the tie-breaking votes.

As of 1979, the European Company Statute is still a proposal. This does not mean that it, therefore, can be ignored. The European Commission is seriously considering implementing this statute in some form in the near future. The European parliament lined up with two-thirds of the delegates in favor of the three-way distribution of power on a corporation's decision-making board. A legalization of the statute would create a series of minimum requirements with which the Member States would have to comply.

Many employers' federations have voiced strong criticisms of the EEC's workers' participation proposal. Most have had experience with some form of workers' participation. They are not convinced that the EEC-type of workers' participation is the best way to improve industrial democracy.

The reaction of multinational companies toward the proposed European Company Statute must be included, as it will affect these corporations the most. Personal interviews with representatives of Philips, Unilever, Enka-Glanzstoff, Hoesch A.G, Akzo, Siemens, and ICI revealed that the statute was considered attractive, but all agreed that it will not be good in practice. The major complaints are that the regulations are too tight, especially with respect to workers' participation, and there is a lack of one harmonious tax system. Each of the above companies considered themselves a worldwide company, and statements such as "we are used to operate in over a hundred countries, so nine do not really make any difference," were heard on occasion.

Dr. Jurgen Steinmetz, General-Council of August Thyssen-Hütte Aktiengesellschaft, best summarized the general consensus among the multinationals in Europe:

> The European Company Statute is in my opinion "a still-born child." Especially if one considers the completely unacceptable arrangement of co-determination, of which the regiments are even worse than in West Germany. Besides the European Company Statute is useless as long as there is no harmonization of tax laws. In conclusion, reality shows that organizations do rather well in international business even without being a European Company.[12]

In conclusion, the European Company Statute, as proposed in 1976, will not receive a warm welcome among international enterprises. None of the corporations are planning to change their organizational structure to become a European Company. A number of the unions are not in favor of the statute. The major fear among unions is that strong national works councils will reduce the unions' strength and importance. Communist unions reject the EEC proposal altogether because they officially turn down any cooperation with management and they are only interested in worker control. Other unions are just not interested and wish to limit their actions to collective bargaining.

The European Commission's major obstacle in implementing the statute will be a harmonization of tax laws. The Member States have different tax systems and rates, and the countries depend on the various systems and rates. The commission has given priority to harmonization of tax laws to facilitate trade among the Member States, but excise duties will also have to be aligned. Without the equalization of duties and taxes, companies pay different rates than their competitors in other nations. The commission wishes to remove any form of distortion of different taxes. The European Company Statute is academic until this is reached. The legal implementation problems are secondary to the fiscal problems. The European Company Statute and a taxation directive will have to be part of the same package. There is a possibility that the commission will accept the European Company Statute for political reasons because it will make a big political splash, but it will not mean anything. It may be that the commission will sit on the taxation directive until they really want the European Company Statute to be used.

FRANCE

In France, enterprise committees (*comités d'entreprise*) must be set up in all organizations employing more than 50 workers.[13] The members of the enterprise committee are elected by the workers. The head of the company is the committee's chairman, and management is required to provide the enterprise committee with full information concerning the state of affairs of the corporation. The French unions are satisfied with the existence of the enterprise committee, and they join their Italian counterparts in rejecting workers' participation at the organization's decision-making level. "Most of the European unions are in favor of worker directors, but the Italians and French are not. The big communist unions in both countries regard worker directors as an undesirable form of collaboration with management, and the socialists too are skeptical."[14]

However, as a result of President Charles de Gaulle's advocacy of workers' participation, works councils in organizations with 50 or more employees do send three representatives to board meetings. These representatives have only a consultative function and have no voting rights. They occupy three seats on the highest administrative board of the enterprise, which can by law be either of the two types of boards: a board of directors (*conseil d'administration*) or a supervisory board (*conseil de surveillance*) and a board of management (*directoire*) combined. The three workers' representatives, of whom one has to be an executive level representative, are elected by the employees.

President Giscard d'Estaing charged a committee, headed by the French industrialist Pierre Sudreau, to examine the problems of the reform of corporate law. In February 1975, the Sudreau Committee published its report on French company law reform. Some of its recommendations are:

1. To require a two-tier board system with a supervisory board and a board of management for all enterprises
2. To increase the number of seats reserved for workers' representatives on the supervisory board to one-third of the total number of seats
3. To provide these workers' representatives with full voting rights
4. To strengthen the consultation that occurs within the enterprise committee

In summary, changes based on the Sudreau Committee's proposals in France's industrial democracy can be expected, especially if one considers that President Giscard d'Estaing favors broadening workers' rights to participation. However, some time will pass, as the unions do not push for co-determination legislation.

AUSTRIA

In Austria, about 70 percent of industry is nationalized and the country's relatively small-scale economy makes it highly dependent upon the world market for its exports. The Austrian Works Council Law of July 1971 gives the Plant Committees the right to be informed by the company on such topics as proposed closures, mergers, layoffs, investments, as well as the profit and loss account and the balance sheet.[15] The philosopy behind the unions' demands was outlined by Wilhelm Hrdlitschka, president of the Chemical Workers' Federation and president of the Austrian Labor Council and Chambers of Labor: "Our demand for co-determination in Austria has as its objective not a change in ownership of the means of production...(but a) democratic balance within the framework of co-determination on an industrial basis."[16] The nationalized companies are not in the forefront of experimentation to improve workers' participation in management.

The 1971 Austrian Law on Plant Committees was amended in 1973 to include co-determination. A third of the supervisory board seats are for workers' representatives. The Austrian workers' participation requirements are almost a replica of the German one-tier system with three exceptions: (1)

the workers' representatives are elected by the works councils; (2) they have no voting rights in appointing the organization's board of management; and (3) it is not possible to appoint outside persons or trade officials to the supervisory board.

IRELAND

There is, in practice, no employees' representation on company boards in Ireland. Internally, in the organization, Irish workers organize in works councils. The legal background to employees' participation is somewhat similar to that in the United Kingdom. However, in Ireland, wage negotiations take place at the national level instead of at the plant or industry level, as in the United Kingdom.

ITALY

Italian workers elect their own delegates to an organization's works council.[17] The interests of the workers are protected by this council, and the Italian unions are satisfied with this arrangement. Just like their French counterparts, the communist-influenced Italian unions do not favor co-determination, and they consider every form of cooperation within an organization between management and workers as an undesirable form of collaboration with capitalism. As a result, no co-determination requirements exist in Italy. Some independently negotiated workers' participation exists at companies such as Fiat and Olivetti, where unions have a strong voice in staffing and investment policies.

The administrative structure for Italian companies calls for three separate bodies: (1) councils of administration (*consiglio d'amministrazione*), which is a relatively large body that is the management of the company, (2) the executive committee (*amministratori delegati*), which is elected by and from among the council of administration and whose task includes the day-to-day operations of the organization, (3) the shareholders' committee (*collegio sindacale*), which is the internal supervisory body empowered to act in the interest of shareholders and third parties; its main function is supervision of the councils of administration.

CONCLUSION

Several West European co-determination requirements and proposals were outlined in this chapter. Changes are expected in the co-determination requirements in the United Kingdom and France based on the Bullock Report and the Sudreau Committee's recommendations respectively. No significant demands for an increase in workers' participation are expected in Italy and Ireland.

The future of all Western European co-determination requirements depends on what happens with the EEC's proposal for a European Company Statute. The interview results revealed that multinationals will not change and become European Companies under the present conditions. However, a legal Europe-wide enforcement of the statute will have an impact upon all national co-determination laws. The European Company Statute is not expected to be implemented in the next few years.

NOTES

1. See: Nancy Foy and Herman Gadon, "Worker Participation: Contrasts in Three Countries," *Harvard Business Review* 54 (May–June 1976):78.

2. Milton Derber, "Crosscurrents in Worker Participation," *Industrial Relations* 9 (February 1970):126.

3. Prospero, "Why BSC's Worker-Director Plan Flopped," *The Director* 24 (February 1972):172.

4. The information of ICI's experiences is based on the author's interviews with Dr. P.G. Harvey, chairman of the Mond Division of ICI and with his staff. These interviews took place in August 1975, in England. The author expresses his sincere thanks to Dr. Harvey and his staff for their helpful suggestions and encouragement.

5. Eric Morgenthaler, "U.K Report, as Expected, Asks Big Firms to Put Labor on the Board," *The Wall Street Journal* (January 27, 1977):7. See also: Neil McInnes, "Boardroom Revolution? In Great Britain, the Rights of Investors Are in Jeopardy," *Barron's* 57 (February 14, 1977):7.

6. Neil McInnes, op. cit., p. 12.

7. The EEC's nine Member States are Belgium, Denmark, Germany, France, Ireland, Italy, Luxembourg, the Netherlands, and the United Kingdom.

8. Commission of the European Communities, *Employees Participation and Company Structure* (Brussels: European Communities, August 1975), p. 12.

9. A part of the data and opinions as expressed by the European Commission in this section are summarized from a personal interview with Mr. Coleman, assistant to Mr. Gundelach, EC Commissioner for internal market affairs. The interview took place on August 12, 1975, in Brussels. The author thanks Mr. Coleman for his help.

10. Edmund Fawcett, "European Companies," *European Community* (July–August 1975):3.

11. Mr. Coleman, European Economic Community, interview, August 12, 1975.

12. From a letter to the author from Dr. Jurgen Steinmetz, General-Council, August Thyssen-Hütte Aktiengesellschaft, August 25, 1976, Duisburg-Hamborn, West Germany. (The translation is by the author.)

13. Sources used for the French section include: Edmond Maire, "France," in *Industry's Democratic Revolution*, ed. Charles Levinson (London: Allen and Urwin, 1974), pp. 324–31; Milton Derber, op. cit., p. 124; Edmund Fawcett, op. cit., p. 4; *U.S. News and World Report* op. cit., p. 85; Prospero, op. cit., p. 172; Commission of the European Communities, op. cit., pp. 66–73; Neil McInnes, "Renault vs. Peugeot," *Barron's* 57 (May 30, 1977):11, 26–27.

14. "Workers on the Board," *The Economist* 246 (March 24, 1973) op. cit., p. 66.

15. Sources used for the Austrian section include: Johannes Schregle, "Forms of Participation in Management," *Industrial Relations* 4 (February 1970): 118–19; Wilhelm Hrdlitschka, "Austria," in *Industry's Democratic Revolution*, ed. Charles Levinson (London: Allen and Unwin, 1974):280–300; *U.S. News and World Report,* op. cit., p. 85; Sam Zagoris, "Policy Implications and Future Agenda," in *The Worker and The Job*, ed. the American Assembly (Englewood Cliffs, N.J.: Prentice Hall, 1974): 117–201.

16. Wilhelm Hrdlitschka, op. cit., pp. 281, 284.

17. Sources used for this section include: S. Benjamin Prasad, "The Growth of Co-determination," *Business Horizons* 20 (April 1977):23–29; Commission of the European Communities, op. cit. pp. 78–84; "Workers on the Board," *The Economist* 246 (March 24, 1973):66.

6

EUROPEAN COMPARATIVE ANALYSIS

A comparative analysis of the statutory requirements and proposals pertaining to co-determination in various European countries and the European Economic Community (EEC) is presented in this chapter. This overview should provide the management of multinational enterprises with an understanding of the constraints and contingencies faced by its subsidiaries while operating in countries with statutory co-determination. The graphical overview of the comparative analysis includes: (1) whether or not a country has statutory co-determination, (2) the statutory administrative structure of the organization, (3) the degree of workers' participation, (4) whether or not the workers' representatives have voting power equal to the shareholders' representatives, and (5) whether or not works councils are required by law.

Most Western European countries require some form of co-determination. As explained earlier, the legal requirements pertaining to workers participating in corporate decision making are often based upon a nation's socioeconomic history. Table 6.1 is the basis for this analysis.

As shown in Table 6.1, countries having legal co-determination requirements include Austria, Denmark, France, West Germany, Luxembourg, Norway, and Sweden. It should be added here that each country has its own requirements. The major differences between the various requirements are included in Table 6.1 and will be discussed here. The EEC, the United Kingdom, and France are considering proposals to implement or extend co-determination. These proposals have been included in Table 6.1 as they have significant implications for multinationals when implemented. There are presently no co-determination requirements in Belgium, Ireland, Italy, the Netherlands, and the United Kingdom. Belgian and Italian unions do not push for co-determination, and Dutch workers have an indirect voice in the election process of the future supervisory board members.

TABLE 6.1. International Comparative Analysis of the Legal Requirements and Proposals Pertaining to Workers' Participation in Various West European Countries.

Countries	Statutory Co-determination?	Administrative Structure of the Board	Division of the Board	Workers' Representatives Equal to Shareholders?	Influence of Workers' Representatives on Appointment of Board of Management?	Works Councils?	Notes
Austria	yes	Supervisory and management board	⅓ workers' and ⅔ shareholders representatives	yes	no	yes	—
Belgium	no	Board of directors	—	—	—	yes	Changes in administrative structure are being studied
Denmark	yes	Supervisory and management board	2 workers' representatives	yes	yes	yes	For companies with 50 or more employees
EEC: European Company Statute (proposal)	yes	Supervisory and management board	⅓ workers' and ⅓ shareholders and ⅓ general interest representatives	yes	yes	yes	for European Companies (EC) only

				Only an advisory status			At least one executive representative on the board; no union interest in co-determination
France (presently)	yes	Supervisory and management board, or only board of directors	3 employees' representatives	Only an advisory status	no	yes	At least one executive representative on the board; no union interest in co-determination
France (Sudreau Committee Proposal)	yes	Supervisory and management board	⅓ workers' and ⅔ shareholders representatives	yes	yes	yes	—
West Germany (companies with 500 to 2,000 employees)	yes	Supervisory and management board	⅓ workers' and ⅔ shareholders representatives	yes	yes	yes	—
West Germany (companies with 2,000 or more employees)	yes	Supervisory and management board	½ workers' and ½ shareholders representatives	yes	yes	yes	At least one of the employees' representatives must be a management employee
Ireland	no	Board of directors	—	—	—	yes	—

67

(continued)

Table 6.1 continued

Countries	Statutory Co-determination?	Administrative Structure of the Board	Division of the Board	Workers' Representatives Equal to Shareholders?	Influence of Workers' Representatives on Appointment of Board of Management?	Works Councils?	Notes
Italy	no	Board of directors	—	—	—	yes	No union interest in co-determination
Luxembourg	yes	Board of directors	⅓ workers' and ⅔ shareholders representatives	yes	yes	yes	Only in large corporations
The Netherlands	no	Supervisory and management board	—	—	—	yes	No direct workers' participation, but indirect voice and veto power over all future supervisory board members
Norway	yes	Corporate assembly (like supervisory board and management board)	⅓ workers' and ⅔ shareholders representatives	yes	yes	yes	Workers' representatives on supervisory board directly appoint ⅓ of board of management

Sweden	yes	Board of directors	2 workers' representatives	yes	yes	yes	Workers' representatives have no voting power in the companies' relations with trade unions; for companies with 100 or more employees
United Kingdom (presently)	no	—	—	—	—	—	Joint consultation for cooperation between management and employees
United Kingdom (Bullock Proposal)	yes	Board of directors	Equal number of workers' and shareholders representatives and several independents	yes	yes	yes	—

Source: Complied by the author.

Nearly all countries with statutory co-determination have limited the requirements to larger companies. For instance, West German companies must have 500 or more workers before they are subject to co-determination, Swedish companies must have 100 or more workers, and in Denmark, companies must have 50 or more workers. A summary of these requirements is included in Table 6.1.

Co-determination takes place at the corporate decision-making level of the corporation. In Table 6.1 a distinction has been made between the two types of administrative structure that are possible at this level in Western European enterprises: (1) board of directors and (2) supervisory board and board of management. The former, which often has an internal structure of supervisory or controlling executives and operation executives, is responsible for managing the company. In the latter, the responsibilities of supervision and day-to-day operations are split between the two boards respectively. Co-determination here will take place at the supervisory board level.

All countries with statutory co-determination, except Sweden and Luxembourg, require corporations to have an administrative structure with a supervisory board and a board of management. Sweden and Luxembourg require a board of directors, and at the present, France permits both structures. The co-determination proposals of France and the EEC call for a structure with a supervisory board and a board of management. The British Bullock proposal calls for a board of directors only.

The degree of workers' participation and whether or not workers' representatives have voting power equal to the shareholders' representatives are major determinants of the implications of co-determination. These two topics are, therefore, included in Table 6.1. Co-determination has a real value for workers only when their voting power is equal to that of the shareholders.

As outlined in Table 6.1, the seats that workers occupy on an organization's corporate decision-making board can be up to 50 percent, as is the case for companies subject to the German Co-determination Act of 1976. However, most workers' representatives have one-third of the seats on a supervisory board, such as in Austria, Luxembourg, Norway, and West Germany for companies with 500 to 2,000 employees. Other types of requirements can be found in Denmark, Sweden, and France, each requiring respectively two, two, and three workers' representatives on the corporate decision-making board. In addition, the Europen Company Statute calls for one-third workers' representatives, one-third shareholders' representatives, and one-third general interest representatives and the British Bullock proposal calls for an equal number of representatives of workers and shareholders and a smaller number of general interest representatives.

Having seats on a board of directors or supervisory board has only significant value if workers' representatives have a voting power equal to that of the shareholders. Therefore, a section has been included in Table 6.1

outlining whether or not this is the case. Workers in Austria, Denmark, West Germany, Luxembourg, Norway, and Sweden do have this equal voting right, which means one equal vote per representative on the board. An exception is France, where three workers' representatives on the board only have an advisory function. The EEC, British, and French proposals for co-determination call for equal voting power on the board.

Another important factor is whether or not the workers' representatives can influence the appointment of the board of management. This is important as the latter is responsible for the corporation's day-to-day operations. As shown in Table 6.1, Denmark, West Germany, Luxembourg, Norway, and Sweden permit this. The Austrian and French workers' representatives on the board cannot vote in matters affecting the board of management. Norway, on the other hand, permits the workers' representatives on the supervisory board to appoint directly one-third of the board of management. The EEC, French, and British proposals provide the workers' representatives with the right to influence the appointment of the board of management by means of equal voting power.

Works councils were among the first industrial relations requirements in most Western European countries. A column is, therefore, included in Table 6.1 to study the extent of the requirements for works councils. In 1978, all Western European countries required works councils, and in some countries these works councils have a significant influence on the election process of the supervisory board. Often, the works councils can propose the candidates for employees' representatives on the board. An exception is the Dutch works councils, which cannot propose candidates, but they have a veto right over all proposed candidates for the supervisory board.

In conclusion, international managers are aware that co-determination affects the operations of multinational enterprises and creates constraints and contingencies for the multinational's subsidiary. To properly control, coordinate, evaluate, and anticipate the subsidiaries' operations, the headquarters must be aware of all co-determination requirements and proposals. However, the international executive will face a variate picture. An attempt has been made in this chapter to present (by means of Table 6.1) a comparative analysis of the co-determination requirements and proposals in Western Europe.

7

WORKERS' PARTICIPATION IN NONDEMOCRATIC SOCIETIES

Workers' participation in managerial decision making can also be found in nondemocratic societies, two of which are analyzed in this chapter (Peru and Yugoslavia). Peru is included because its requirements might be a reference model for possible future representation demands in Latin America. Yugoslavia is included as its participation model may be considered representative of Eastern European countries.

YUGOSLAVIA

No changes occurred in Yugoslavia's postwar economic position, and the country remained an underdeveloped, agrarian country in which 75 percent of the population lived on agriculture. To improve this situation, the Yugoslavian government decided not to strengthen its centralized power and influence, which had produced harmful effects in other socialist countries, but to implement a self-management system.[1] After a period of a centralized economy, with almost no participation of the citizens, the government introduced a self-management system in organizations. The ownership of the means of production was transferred in 1950 from the government to the workers employed by each particular organization.

Social, as opposed to state-ownership over the means of production, is one of the cornerstones of workers' self-management. The essence of social ownership over the means of production is reflected in the fact that capital assets are entrusted for direct management to the workers who operate them in their own interests and in the interest of the social community. Bearing in mind that nobody, except society as a whole, has the right of ownership over the socially owned means of production—neither the socio-political community, nor the enterprise, nor the individual worker is allowed any legal ownership basis to appropriate the product of the socially owned means of production, or independently to determine the conditions of the income distribution.[2]

This means that workers, by accepting employment in a particular organization, have the right to participate in the decision-making processes in the organization. The workers collectively have the right to use the means of production. In exchange, the organization will have to make an annual payment to society as a whole.

Since the early 1950s, attempts have been made by the Yugoslavian government to reduce its role in the economic section of society. Decisions concerning an organization's investments were made until 1960 by the federal government. Responsibility for the investment decisions was transferred to the regional government level in 1960. In 1965, the change from a centralized to a decentralized decision-making process was completed. The individual organization has sole responsibility for its investments and distribution of income decisions.[3]

The move from federal central planning to planning at the organizational level resulted in a decrease of the economic organization's dependency upon the federal government. Before, production quotas were determined by the government. However, the organization is now allowed to set production levels and prices according to the demand and supply for goods and services.

The worker self-management system, hastily launched in 1950 by Marshal Tito, is based on the philosophy that labor-management presupposes self-government by the workers and assumes that each firm will be guided by the desires of its employees.[4] "That is, the legal control to manage the enterprise rests with the employees of each economic unit, known under the 1974 constitution as a Basic Organization of Associated Labor (BOAL). Each complete economic function forms its own BOAL."[5] The total economic organization is subdivided in economic or work units of associated labor. The workers of each economic or work unit elect their unit's works council, which is responsible for the supervision of the day-to-day operations of the economic or work unit and makes decisions concerning investments and reorganization.[6]

When an economic organization consists of several economic or work units, indirect management is carried out through the unit's works councils at the unit level and through a central works council at the organization's policy-formulating and decision-making level. The central works council is the highest decision-making element in the organization. All workers of all economic or work units in an economic organization are allowed to vote for the members of the central works council. This council approves the organization's annual report, has the final word in investment and reorganization decisions, and appoints the business board and general manager. The latter two are responsible for the day-to-day operations of the organization. The business board is often elected from the ranks of the organization's workers who have performed well in their field of specialty.[7]

There are advisory committees at every managerial level of the organization. Their task is to become more closely and thoroughly acquainted with problems and to provide management with proposals and/or advice. Members of advisory committees are appointed by the unit's works councils or the central works council, depending on the committee's duties.

The question arises, how do workers perceive the self-management system in Yugoslav enterprises, and is it successful?

> Whether or not self-management has really worked can be gauged by different means. Examination of the 1967–75 output figures and jobless rates for Yugoslavia indicated that the people are economically better off. This is not to say that Yugoslavia has emerged as a rich country under the system. It is still poor; the per capita gross national product is about $850 a year. If the purchasing power as well as the expenditure patterns are factoral, the standard of living is about a third of the American average and comparable to that of Mexico.[8]

Results of opinion polls in 1971 pointed to a mood of bitter and resentful apprehension among the workers toward self-management. Workers in Yugoslavia were not against the self-management system as such, but they thought that much was wrong in the way it was practiced. In reality, it was found that discussions and debates took place in the works councils; however, only a small percentage of all decisions actually taken represent a democratic "self-management" judgment.[9] A major reason for the reduction of the workers' input in the self-management system resulted from government attempts to stimulate the economy when economic growth halted around 1966. The stimulation plan included methods to increase domestic and international competition, resulting in unemployment in the less competitive industries. Socially or politically oriented plans of the central works councils could not be implemented as a result of the shift toward a competitive market place. Decisions had to be based on sound economic investment grounds to meet the competition.

A reaction to this situation occurred in 1973 with development of the labor control concept. The purpose of an organization's labor control group is to execute control over the management organs of the organization. Included are topics such as implementation of works councils' self-management rights. The new concept of labor control is still in the early development stage, and problems occur during the implementation.

In summary, the degree to which Yugoslavian self-management should be considered a success fully depends upon the sources used for a possible analysis. It is safe to say that the system was working satisfactorily for the

Yugoslav workers during a period of strong economic growth. However, since the stagnation in the economic growth, workers developed negative feelings toward the self-management system. This resulted in the implementation of labor control groups to supervise the organization's management organs.

PERU

Peru is the only country in Latin America with statutory workers' participation. It is included in this study because it can well be an example of future requirements in its neighboring countries. There has not been much written on the subject because the Peruvian project is relatively new and sources of information are further reduced as very little is written in English.

In October 1968, a military junta overthrew the government of President Belaunde in Peru. The military junta ousted President Belaunde for several reasons: Belaunde erased the Peruvian government's claim of 150 million dollars against the International Petroleum Company (a Standard Oil of New Jersey subsidiary), spiraling inflation, and a growing gap between the "haves" and the "have nots."[10] The military regime, led by Velasco Alvarado, sought to decrease the disparity in incomes and to increase Peru's economic independence through the creation of industrial communities (*comunidades industriales*). The industrial communities were created by Decree-Law 18350 on July 27, 1970. "The Government's declared purpose was to increase productivity and capital formation and encourage the participation of workers in the profits, property and direction of industrial firms and promote the social, cultural, professional and technical development of the workers."[11] Industrial communities must be organized in all industrial concerns employing six or more full-time employees. However, the decree-law is for the most part not clearly defined.

In Decree-Law 18384, the Peruvian government spelled out objectives of an industrial community:

1. To strengthen the industrial undertaking by the unitary action of the workers in management, in the production process, in the property of the undertaking and in reinvestment, and by means of stimulating constructive forms of interrelation between capital and labor
2. To unify the workers' action in the management of the industrial undertaking in order to safeguard its rights and interests as guaranteed to them by Legislative Decree No. 18350 as participators in ownership
3. To administer the assets they receive, for the workers' benefits
4. To promote the workers' social, cultural, occupational and technical development[12]

A general assembly of the full-time workers of an organization (managers included) is the first step in instituting an industrial community.[13] At this general assembly meeting, an organizing committee is appointed to draft a constitution and procedural rules and to obtain legal ratification from the government. After these tasks are performed, the industrial community convenes for its first meeting. In the initial meeting, a council is elected to achieve the general assembly's objectives. The council members are (1) elected for a two-year term, (2) not permitted a successive term, (3) receive no additional pay, (4) work as council members on their own time, (5) not permitted any direct ownership in the firm, and (6) cannot currently be union officials.

The council selects one individual from its membership to represent the industrial community on the company's board of directors. This person sits on the board for a period of one year. The council is also responsible for the management of the funds that the industrial community receives from the company. Under the decree, a company must relinquish 15 percent of its net profits before taxes to the industrial community. The industrial community is required by law to use these funds to acquire stock in the company until it becomes half owner of the company. If the company does not issue any new stock, then the present stockholders are required to sell their shares to the industrial community.

If the company falls into the public category, then the funds must be used to acquire the organization's bonds; if the company does not have any bonds, then the funds must be used to buy government bonds. The industrial community must invest until it obtains a bond value equal to 50 percent of the corporation's value in assets.

When an industrial community obtains half ownership in the company, it then distributes shares to its members on the basis of seniority. Shares may only be redeemed by the employees to whom they were issued in the event that their employment is terminated. It should be clarified that employees hold stock in the industrial community and not in the company. This means that the workers have no direct say in the company, but that they are represented through the council. Dividends on the industrial community's shares are distributed to all full-time employees who have worked with the company for at least one year. Half of the dividends are equally distributed to all employees, and the other half is distributed on the basis of seniority with the company.

After half ownership of the company is achieved, the industrial community may use the company's annual payment for anything except dispersing it to its members or buying stock in a company which is not expanding. The industrial community has to distribute new shares to the members every five years to reflect the gains accumulated in the past five years. The shares are allocated on the previously mentioned seniority basis.

Analysis

The industrial community idea in Peru is unlike any other in the world.[14] The Peruvian idea fosters employee loyalty, as it ties distribution of dividends to seniority in the company. It also provides a gradual transition period by linking the transfer of ownership to the funds distributed to the industrial communities. Thus, by limiting the industrial community's inflow of funds to 15 percent of the company's net profit before taxes, the transition period will be gradual and will provide ample time for both the company and the employees to adjust to the new situation.

One of the important foundations of the Peruvian idea is the industrial community's obligation to buy stock in the company until it is half owner. This requirement allows the employees to see a definite link between their production efforts and their remuneration. They gain ownership in the company quicker by generating a higher net profit before taxes. Also, under the Peruvian concept, workers receive a share of the dividends that the industrial community receives.

Like any other revolutionary concept, the Peruvian idea has had its difficulties. The biggest problem has been the interpretation of the law. Problems, such as determination of the company's stock value, have plagued the implementation of the new law. A company can also postpone the increase of stockholdings by its industrial community by annually expanding at a growth rate of 15 percent or more, since 15 percent is the amount by which an industrial community invests back in the host company. Owners can also circumvent the requirements by having a commercial enterprise as well as a plant, whereby they can incur a loss at the plant by selling goods from the plant at a discount to their commercial enterprise. This transfer of profits allows the owners to prevent the industrial community from increasing its ownership at the plant. Another problem arises when an industrial community has half ownership and there is a stalemate to select a chairman of the board. This may have implications for the efficiency of the organization.

The Peruvian government has issued laws to close some of the above loopholes and has decided that it will appoint the chairman of the board in the event of a stalemate.[15] In addition, the government tries to increase employees' knowledge of the law and the working of the business enterprise. Under direction of the Peruvian labor department, workers attend seminars and classes to achieve these objectives. The Peruvian government currently is revising its education program to make it more meaningful and useful to the workers.

At this time, it is too early to tell if the Peruvian idea is successful or not, but once the law is thoroughly understood by all parties and the educational level of the workers has been improved, then the Peruvian idea should have little trouble functioning.

CONCLUSION

The statutory workers' participation requirements in Peru and Yugoslavia have been outlined and analyzed in this chapter. No evidence is available that the workers' participation plans of these nondemocratic societies result in either increased productivity or job satisfaction. Opinion polls in 1971 in Yugoslavia revealed that workers were not satisfied with the execution of the self-management system.

On several occasions, it has been suggested that the Yugoslavian government did assist the Peruvian regime in the design of the industrial community. There are no known sources that discuss this possible relationship, and a comparison of the requirements of each country does not show many similarities.

There is a fundamental difference between the Western European co-determination concept and the workers' participation requirements in both Yugoslavia and Peru. The ownership of the means of production is the central point. In Western Europe, workers can participate in the decision-making process concerning the use of the organization's capital assets. However, the ownership of the means of production remains with the organization's shareholders.

The Yugoslavian self-management system is based on social ownership. This means that the capital assets are entrusted for direct management to the workers, but society as a whole has the legal right of ownership over the means of production.

Only in Peru can workers indirectly own up to 50 percent of their organization. Companies must relinquish 15 percent of their net profits before taxes annually to the industrial communities. The latter is required to use these funds to acquire stock in the company until it owns 50 percent of the company. The industrial community is owned and managed by the company's workers.

In summary, the West European and Yugoslavian workers do not own part of the means of production. The shareholder and society at large respectively own the capital assets. Peruvian workers, on the other hand, can own indirectly up to 50 percent of the company.

NOTES

1. Milan Rukanvina, "Yugoslavia," in *Industry's Democratic Revolution,* ed. Charles Levinson (London: Allen and Unwin, 1974), p. 155.

2. Ibid., p. 160.

3. See also: Wiardi Beckman Stichting, *Op weg naar Arbeiderzelfbestuur* (Deventer, Holland: Kluwer, 1974), pp. 112–13.

4. S. Benjamin Prasad, "The Growth of Co-determination," *Business Horizons* 20 (April 1977):25–26.

5. Ibid., p. 26.

6. Literature used to obtain information on the Yugoslav self-management system requirements included: Milan Rukavina, op. cit. pp. 153–86; Wiardi Beckman Stichting, op. cit.; R.M. Boonzaijer Flaes, "Abeiderscontrole in Joegoslavie," *Intermediair* 11 (August 15, 1975):11–15; Janez Jerovsek, "Self-management System in Yugoslav Enterprises," *Industrial Relations* 15 (February 1975):113–22; S. Benjamin Prasad, op. cit., pp. 25–7; "Who Manages Whom," *The Economist* 24 (August 21, 1971):22–25; Josip Obredovic, "Participation and Work Attitudes in Yugoslavia," *Industrial Relations* 9 (February 1970):161–69; Bogdan Denitch, "The Relevance of Yugoslav Self-Management," in *Comparative Communism*, ed. Gary K. Bertsch and Thomas W. Ganschow (San Francisco: W.H. Freeman and Company, 1976), pp. 268–81.

7. For a good description of the operation of a Yugoslavian enterprise see: Elliot Carlson, "Participation—Yugoslavian Style," *International Management* 128 (April 1973):74–82.

8. Prasad, op. cit., p. 27.

9. *The Economist*, op. cit., p. 22.

10. Donald W. Pearson, "The Communidad Industrial: Peru's Experiment in Worker Management," *Inter-American Economic Affairs* 27 (Summer 1973):17.

11. Richard D. Robinson, "The Peruvian Experiment," unpublished paper, The Sloan School of Management, Massachusetts Institute of Technology, April 1976, p. 24.

12. Luis Pasora and Jorge Santistovan, "Industrial Communities and Trade Unions in Peru: A Preliminary Analysis," *International Labor Review* 18 (August–September 1973):128.

13. The description of the Peruvian Decree-Law 18384 and its implications are summarized from: Pearson, op. cit. pp. 17–31; Robinson, op. cit.; and Pasora and Santistovan, op. cit. pp. 127–42.

14. This analysis is based on: Pearson, op. cit. pp. 17–31; Robinson, op. cit.; Pasora and Santistovan, op. cit. pp. 127–42.

15. Robinson, op. cit., p. 30; Also see: Wm. Foote Whyte and Giorgio Alberti, "The Industrial Community in Peru," *The Annals* 431 (May 1977):103–12.

8

ANALYSIS OF CO-DETERMINATION EFFECTS

INTRODUCTION

The effects of co-determination are analyzed in this chapter. Co-determination, as required by law in most European countries, has impact upon organizations, managements, employees, unions, and society. To present a comprehensive overview of the major effects of co-determination, the chapter is subdivided into sections. Tables 8.1 and 8.2 provide a summary of the findings. The majority of the information is based on personal interviews with representatives of both subsidiaries of multinationals and companies in Europe.[1]

UNION POWER

It is suggested that co-determination will increase the power of the unions in society. European unions are organized at the local, district, or national level and not at the level of the individual organization or industry, such as in the United States. This means that in Europe, collective bargaining takes place at either the local, district, or national level. The co-determination laws permit unions to either occupy seats on a company's supervisory board or propose supervsory board members. The aggregate of these union-appointed or union-oriented supervisory board members all over the region or country influences the collective bargaining processes to the disadvantage of corporations. The unions are now represented on both sides of the bargaining table. The co-determination laws do not result in a better distribution of power among unions and shareholders, but rather in its concentration in the hands of the trade unions.

An internal study of the German Federation of Trade Unions (DGB) underlines that the coordination of all power positions will result in a situation where the unions influence the total economic system of West Germany.[2] "The unions are not, as they openly admit, aiming at improvement of the workers' lot, but rather the fundamental re-distribution of power within human society in favor of the unions."[3] This increase in union power will have an effect upon the free enterprise system as a whole, since the unions will obtain a strong and influential voice in the decision-making processes of not only the government, but also private enterprises. "This could change our economic system from a socially oriented market economy to an economy centrally controlled by the trade unions,"[4] says Gilbert Kley, member of the Management Board of Siemens AG and member of the Presidential Board of Confederation of German Employers' Associations (BDA).

Twenty-seven German managers and 15 German workers' representatives of 20 and 12 different companies respectively in West Germany reacted to the author's statement 1: "Co-determination will result in a centralization of power within human society in favor of the trade unions." Of the German managers, 74 percent agreed, while 60 percent of the workers' representatives disagreed. However, it is interesting that one-third of workers' representatives did agree with the statement (see Table 8.1).

The power of the unions is not to be underestimated as shown in the following cases: (1) A leader of a single union and his associates can occupy seats on supervisory boards of more than one company. For example, Mr. Eugen Loderer, the head of West Germany's giant metal workers' union, I.G. Metall, occupies a seat as vice-president on the supervisory board of Volkswagen (V.W.). Mr. Loderer also sits on the board of the Mannesmann Steel Pipe Company, and his I.G. Metall union associates sit in the board rooms of most of the other large German steel and auto companies.[5] Imagine a

TABLE 8.1. Frequency of Responses to Statement 1.

	German Managers		Workers' Representatives	
	No.	%	No.	%
Strongly agree	5	18.5	0	0
Agree	15	55.5	5	33.3
Undecided	3	11	1	6.7
Disagree	2	7.5	2	13.3
Strongly disagree	2	7.5	7	46.7
Total	27	100	15	100

Source: Compiled by the author.

situation whereby the president of the UAW occupies seats on the boards of directors of both General Motors and United States Steel and his associates occupy seats on the boards of directors of Ford, Chrysler, and Bethlehem Steel Corporation. (2) The DGB also owns companies in West Germany including the largest construction company, the fourth largest bank, one of the largest life insurance companies, newspapers, and several other corporations. It is possible, for instance in the insurance industry, that a shareholders' representative, representing the owners on the supervisory board of a union-owned insurance company, is at the same time a workers' representative on the supervisory board of a competitive insurance company. Mr. H.O. Vetter is chairman of the supervisory board of the union-owned *Volksfürsorge-Lebensversicherung* in Hamburg and he is there a representative of the major stockholder, the DGB. It is possible for him or his associates to occupy, at the same time, a seat as employees' representative on the supervisory board of *AllianzLeben* or any other competitive life insurance company. The same situation could develop in the health insurance industry.[6]

Again, this example can be related to the United States. The AFL-CIO unions own Union Labor Life Insurance Company (ULLICO). Imagine a situation whereby the union-owned ULLICO's competitors, such as Occidental Life, are required to accept workers' representatives on the board who are at the same time shareholders' representatives on ULLICO's board. A different example for the United States could be a situation whereby a member of the board of directors of radio station WCFL, which is owned and operated by the Chicago Federation of Labor and Industrial Union Council, occupies a seat on a competitive radio station's board of directors. A conflict of interest will exist, especially in decision-making situations affecting competition.

In summary, co-determination results in an increase in union power in society. The facts that union leaders occupy seats on the supervisory boards of competing companies and occupy seats both on boards of union-owned corporations and their competitive companies at the same time result in conflict of interest situations.

CO-DETERMINATION: A MEANS TO REDUCE UNION POWER?

Co-determination results in an increased involvement of workers in the decision-making processes of an organization. The works councils, through which the workers participate at all levels of the organization, especially increase the workers involvement. This increase in the works councils' stature may even result in a reduction of union power among workers. Management can increase the works councils' stature even more by providing them with additional data and a supportive attitude, thereby reducing the union's power to a minimum.

To investigate whether or not corporations use this tactic, managers and representatives of employers' associations were asked, "Should management promote a strong internal works council to reduce the union's power?" Representatives of the Dutch confederation of employers' associations (VNO) stated that a corporation has to make sure it can both cooperate with its workers in a good relationship and work with the unions. Both should be considered very desirable. They explained: "Strong works councils will reduce the power of the unions, but this can backfire, as it means that unions lose contact with their members and have to become extreme to obtain the grip again. In the end, you will lose more ground than you would have with a normal relationship."[7]

Representatives of Unilever, Philips, ICI, Hoesch, AKZO, Opel, Mobil, Bayer, BASF, and several other corporations explained that it is not a policy in their company to increase the works councils' power at the expense of the unions and that they are all considering it in their own best interest to create a good relationship with both unions and works councils. However, several company representatives added that other companies might use this tactic to reduce the role of the unions.

A representative of a major electronics company in Germany acknowledged that quite a number of companies will try to increase the works councils' power at the expense of the union's power. He explained:

> Unions developed next to the works councils and conflicts do exist. I don't think you want to kill the unions but you should tell them not to hinder the works council, and the company should not hinder the union. A distribution of tasks is important. The whole system corrects the unions, and the works councils are often more cooperative. When the unions lose contact with their members, they will adjust.[8]

A DGB representative acknowledged the possible threat to the union's power and confirmed that on several occasions unions had lost considerable power within organizations. Over time, this loss of power had returned and stabilized at the previous level.

STALEMATES AND COMPROMISES?

Problems may arise during the voting process on a supervisory board, especially in those organizations subject to parity co-determination. In the joint supervisory board membership, the often opposing interests of shareholders and workers face each other. Co-determination can undermine the functions expected to be fulfilled by an enterprise in our free economic order. This system—based on private property—requires immediate reactions of the entrepreneurs to changing conditions in the market place. Stalemate situations in the voting process on the supervisory board can block quick decisions and adaptations.

Private enterprises often depend on fast decisions. Increasing international competition and constant technological change necessitate a management that can make its decisions fast and efficiently. When a stalemate situation occurs in the voting process on the supervisory board, decisions are delayed or made possible only by concessions. The BDA suggested that:

> Parity co-determination in the coal and steel industries has not stood the test; on controversial issues decisions were postponed because the neutral man, in the face of block votes of the two parties (shareholder–labor) of equal strength, often was not prepared to bear the responsibility for the "casting vote."[9]

The DGB does not agree with the above statement. They argue that compromises do not happen under parity co-determination as required in the coal, iron, and steel industries and that the neutral man is often the mediator. Dieter Henning, worker-supervisory board member of Mannesmannrohren-Werke answered in the following manner to the question, "Do you have a lot of stalemates?"

> Before co-determination, decisions were made considering only economic points of view. Now the interests of the employees are taken into account since management knows quite well that there are ten worker representatives on the superviory board. Proposals are drawn up in such a way that they are likely to be passed by the whole board; there aren't many actual disputes in voting because many problems have been cleared up beforehand. The supervisory board is clever enough to know that it requires the agreement of the workers and adapts to this fact. When there is a fundamental disagreement, the neutral member must try to obtain a compromise.[10]

The above was confirmed by the Biedenkopf Commission, a government appointed group that studied co-determination. Next to no evidence of stalemates in decision making at the supervisory board was found by this commission, the major reason being that decisions were screened and discussed with the works councils before bringing them before the supervisory board.

Several problems are inherent in Germany's Co-determination Act of 1976. There is no provision in the law for a neutral board member, which means that there are equal numbers of representatives of employees and shareholders; there is no neutral member present to break the tie. However, to solve a possible stalemate, the law provides that the chairman of the board has an additional vote to break the tie.

Table 8.2 provides an overview of the frequency of responses to statement #2: "Stalemates on the supervisory board subject to co-determination will be...." Of the 20 interviewed German managers of 20 different German companies or U.S. susidiaries, 60 percent felt that stalemates will often or almost always be a problem. The majority of the 14 interviewed German workers' representatives of 12 different companies considered stalemates to be very seldom a problem or not a problem (see Table 8.2).

Co-determination sometimes can result in stalemate situations, which could endanger the efficiency of the organization as a whole, as decisions will be delayed. Another factor to be considered is the increase of the demands on management time, patience, understanding, and skills, particularly in group discussions and so on, as managers will have to spend more time explaining and discussing the topics under consideration. It should be questioned if these discussions are not an unnecessary diversion of management resources at a time when most companies are faced with strong international competition and rapidly advancing technological changes.

WORKERS AND CO-DETERMINATION

While discussing a topic so closely related to labor, it is necessary to analyze the perception of workers toward co-determination. The discussion here is centered around the question, "Is labor really interested in co-determination?" This should be considered the principal topic of this section, as the outcome will affect the efficiency of the organization as a whole. Answering the above question, Mr. Coleman, representative of the European Economic Community (EEC), used an example to underline the EEC Commission's feeling that workers are, indeed, interested in co-determination. Mr. Coleman states, "In Denmark over fifty percent of the organization's employees have to vote in favor of co-determination before it must be implemented.... in eighty percent

TABLE 8.2. Frequency of Responses to Statement 2.

	Management		Workers' Representatives	
Almost always a problem	4	20	0	0
Often a problem	8	40	0	0
Occasionally a problem	6	30	5	35.7
Very seldom a problem	2	10	8	57
Not a problem	0	0	1	7.3
Total	20	100	14	100

Source: Compiled by the author.

of the organizations eligible for co-determination employees voted in favor of workers' participation and the ratio was seventy to thirty percent in favor."[11]

The BDA stated that workers are not really interested in co-determination, and a 1966 survey by an independent social research institute (EMNID-Institut) confirmed this. The results of the study showed also that workers subject to the German Works Constitution Act of 1952 (one-third workers' representation on the supervisory board) were more satisfied with their total work climate than workers in the coal, iron, and steel industry with parity co-determination.[12] In addition, it was reported in 1974 that "the average worker in Europe does not care very much for board representation, and he does not expect any remarkable improvement of his own situation to result from such representation."[13]

In an attempt to measure the workers' attitudes toward co-determination, this author, in 1975, asked 23 workers of five German companies to rank their priorities. The same list of possible interests as used in the EMNID-Institut study of 1966 was provided to the interviewees. Table 8.3 represents the order of importance of the interests as expressed by the workers. The first column represents this author's findings in 1975. The second and third columns have been included for comparison reasons; they represent the findings of the 1966 EMNID-Institut study.[14] The second column was the result for organized workers and the third column for nonorganized workers. The author did not distinguish between these two groupings as the sample size was small (N=23) (see Table 8.3). The first column should not be considered an exact representation of the perception toward co-determination among all German workers.

TABLE 8.3. Ranking of German Workers' Interests.

	1975	1966 (Organized workers)	1966 (Nonorganized workers)
Job security	1	4	3
General social security	2	1	1
Longer pay leave	3	3	2
Higher wages and thirteenth month's pay	4	2	4
Reduction in work hours	5	7	7
Workers' share of capital	6	5	6
Better training	7	6	5
Increase in co-determination	8	8	8

Source: Compiled by the author and the EMNIO-INSTITUTE.

The sample size was too small. However, it does provide an indication of the opinions of randomly chosen workers. A comparison of the 1966 and the 1975 figures shows an increase in interest in job security. This can be explained by the fact that the world economy was in a recession stage in 1975 and workers were mostly interested in keeping their jobs. No major differences were found, and interest in co-determination was still lowest on the list of priorities.

Executives were also asked how they perceived the workers' interests in co-determination. The thrust of most answers was the same, and it was best expressed by Mr. Haighton, Department of Personnel and Industrial Relations, Europe, Philips N.V.:

> It is a difficult question. It is often that the minority of workers are better motivated and informed. I think that in general there are large groups that are insufficiently connected with workers' participation and do not know what is going on. They do not see a relationship with their immediate job environment. Plus I think we can do more positive things at the shop floor level. The unions want to participate, but we (management) think the shop floor level is more important.[15]

Dr. Ivo van Haren, member of the supervisory board of AKZO Nederland B.V., adds to this, "Workers' representatives are too far from the workers, and the works councils provide better communication. One should start implementing participative management at the bottom instead of at the top."[16]

With every type of participative management, only a small percentage of the workers is really involved. In many decisions—no matter how important to labor relations—only a few workers are directly involved. Real involvement, effective participation, and communication are processes which occur in the work place centered around a task to be performed or an object to be achieved.

Dr. P.G. Harvey of Imperial Chemical Industries outlined his experience that workers wish to participate by making contributions relevant to their work experiences. Imperial Chemical Industries' management was asked by the shop stewards to explain the process by which management arrived at an investment decision. The process was explained to them, and management asked the shop stewards at what stage in the process they thought workers should participate.

> Their reply was that they believed they had a real contribution to make, from the point of sanctioning the decision, on such matters as the location of the plant, who would construct it, the conditions of employment, the layout, and the social systems that would match the technical systems of the plant. They were quite clear in assigning to management and those with specified skills, the earlier stages determining the justification of the project leading up to sanction. In other words, they were saying they wished to participate by making a contribution relevant to their work experience.[17]

The 23 interviewed German workers were asked to describe their major complaints with respect to co-determination. Over 70 percent of these workers were disappointed with the effects of co-determination. The main complaint was that the workers did not feel related to the decision-making process on the supervisory board or even to the employees' representatives on the board. The workers had a more positive attitude toward the works councils, which allowed them to be informed and to participate at the shopfloor level. The interviews revealed also that in many cases, workers' representatives are brushed off by co-workers on the grounds that they are on management's side now.

Workers do not feel directly involved in co-determination, as unions often propose or appoint workers' representatives or the election process goes via an electoral college. Another problem is the lack of monetary incentives. To obtain a positive attitude toward co-determination, the unions in Europe are studying the possibility of connecting monetary incentives to co-determination. These incentives would have to be provided by the corporation. The employers' federation oppose these plans as they consider it unfair that stockholders would have to provide monetary incentives to workers to encourage them to participate in corporate decision making.

In summary, the unions in Europe, the EEC, and the more radical workers state that co-determination has top priority among all workers. The BDA contradicts this. Research data gathered in 1966 by the EMNID-Institut and in 1975 by the author confirm that the average worker does not care much for board representation. Major reasons behind this apathy are the lack of both real workers' involvement in co-determination and monetary incentives. It was found that in most cases the workers are more interested in participation at the shopfloor level than at the corporate decision-making level.

WHITE COLLAR WORKERS BYPASSED

Managerial employees at the middle and upper ranks in the organization subject to co-determination are frustrated and they see themselves as seriously threatened by co-determination. These employees are bypassed in most co-determination models and are often excluded from the communication process. Co-determination requirements, except for the German Co-determination Act of 1976, normally exclude middle and upper management from the joint decision-making process, as they do not belong to a union.

The unions are not willing to accommodate the upper and middle level employees because they fear that the latter will support and vote with the stockholders' representatives, which would seriously threaten the struggle for union power. As a result, these employees aim at independent representation of their collective interests, and white collar workers are organizing in unions to protect their interests. This happens especially in high white–collar-oriented industries such as insurance and banking.

The basic requirement for union leaders on the supervisory board as representatives of the blue collar workers is not justifiable in, for instance, the banking and insurance industries. Reasons for this are that personnel in these industries consists of mostly clerical workers and managers and these employees have a low degree of unionization. The inherent nature of these industries does not require a large number of blue collar workers. Mainly lower and middle management personnel are employed by banks and insurance companies. These employees are, in general, not unionized. There are companies where there is nearly no unionization, and to demand by law that union leaders represent these employees on the supervisory board does not seem appropriate since they have chosen not to join these unions.

COMPETENCY OF WORKERS' REPRESENTATIVES

Workers or their representatives on the works councils and supervisory board must have sufficient business knowledge to participate in decision making. Persons opposed to co-determination feel that workers or their representatives have a too limited basic business knowledge. The latter are perceived to be incapable of discussing in-depth problems related to the organization, market research, production planning, and investments, especially at the corporate decision-making level. The unions realized this possible problem at an early stage during the implementation of works councils and they developed training programs.

The following statements show that the unions have either been rather successful in training the workers or the workers have a rather good understanding of business problems, maybe as a result of a high degree of motivation. The management of Philips considers the level of business knowledge among the members of the works councils as "not a big problem, especially in a big organization where there are plenty of knowledgeable people with experience."[18] Mr. De Bijll Nachenius of Unilever agrees with respect to Unilever's experience with works councils: "We found quite a good level of knowledge, especially where higher personnel gets involved."[19] Dr. Ivo van Haren of AKZO adds: "If the works councils are to work well, then the workers elect the most suitable members. But there is a danger that the most popular screamer gets elected over the most competent person."[20] No negative remarks were heard in Germany with respect to the level of knowledge of the workers' representatives on the supervisory boards. On several occasions, these representatives were praised.

Twenty-five executives of 21 companies in Europe responded to statement

#3: "Workers' representatives have a too limited business knowledge and experience to contribute in the decision-making process." Disagreement was found in 64 percent of the executives, who were also satisfied with the workers' representatives's performance (see Table 8.4).

The only problem in big multinationals is language. To accommodate all directors, some of whom are from abroad, the discussion language is English. Not all workers' representatives speak that language, however.

In conclusion, managements of most organizations in Europe are satisfied with the level of knowledge of the workers' representatives. The latter will have a better understanding of the internal problems of the organization and can more easily obtain information than management. However, the workers' representatives might miss the external experience. Additional training and motivation will assist the workers' representatives in the decision-making processes, but it should be added that it is a profession to be a manager, which requires knowledge and experience, and one cannot join the ranks at once.

IMPACT ON COLLECTIVE BARGAINING

The managements of companies in Western Europe fear the effects of co-determination on the collective bargaining processes. All of the interviewed executives included this topic among the major problems they expect as a result of co-determination.

Employers and unions have to consider different interests in collective bargaining. Under the pressure of competition in the market place, companies must remain competitive, and the degree of achieving this is measured in profitability. Closely related with this is the long-term survival of the company and often a justification of its existence. The employers must observe the

TABLE 8.4. Frequency of Responses to Statement 3.

	Managers	
	No.	%
Strongly agree	2	8
Agree	5	20
Undecided	2	8
Disagree	12	48
Strongly disagree	4	16
Total	25	100

Source: Compiled by the author.

profitability of the organization, and in this context, wages are costs which reduce the profitability.

Unions, on the other hand, represent the interests of the workers and they must obtain job security and the largest possible benefits for these workers during collective bargaining. Job security can only be guaranteed when a corporation is profitable and has a long-term survival chance. The profitability of the corporation is, therefore, of interest to the workers. However, this interest changes when the profitability has reached a point where workers perceive to have job security. Then unions will demand increases in workers' benefits. A worker-director on the board of management of Hoesch A.G. was asked how he evaluates the relationship between social and economic interests in a declining economy. His answer was, "Our first objective is to protect the job by not increasing demands. When there is an economic boom then we will demand wage increases. The union adjusts itself and the workers are fully informed."[21] This question was asked of 15 workers' representatives on supervisory boards, and 80 percent of the answers were in a similar trend.

A compromise between the employers' and the unions' interests should be the result of the collective bargaining process. A fair compromise can only be reached if the bargaining parties are of equal strength and are independent of each other. The unions contend that without co-determination there has never been and never will be equal strength between the bargaining parties. They feel that the corporations' power is variable and depends on several factors such as the industry in which the company operates, the possibility of capital movements, foreign investments, and so on. The employers' federations disagree with the unions and argue that co-determination will result in an imbalance of strength to the disadvantage of the employers.

An awkward situation arises when collective bargaining takes place between a company's board of management and the unions representing the company's workers. It is possible that one or more members of the board of management are or feel dependent upon the employees' representatives on their supervisory board for reappointment. These board of management members are involved in conflict of interest situations. As a board of management member, they are responsible for the well-being of the organization and its profitability; however, for employment they may be indirectly dependent upon the representatives of unions and workers. As a result they may favor labor interests. Another rather peculiar situation can develop in nationwide or industrywide collective bargaining between unions and employers' associations, as is commonly done in Europe. Board of management executives of several companies will form the collective bargaining group for the employers' association. Again, the situation might arise that one or more of these board of management members on the employers' associations' collective bargaining group are or feel dependent upon the workers' representatives on the supervisory board of their organization for reappointment. It is possible that they favor labor interests, and this will result in a situation where the unions sit on both sides of the bargaining table.

In summary, co-determination will affect the collective bargaining process. Both parties, unions and employers' federations, admit that a conflict will exist between co-determination and the collective bargaining process. No longer are the parties involved equally or independently of each other.

RELAXING OF TENSION

A projected or possible advantage of increased employees' participation is the relaxing of tension between labor and management. Increased participation may be beneficial to the company as well as to the workers. Dr. P.G. Harvey of the Imperial Chemical Industries stated, "The most important result, which is not readily quantified, is the possibility of a changing relationship between management and employees."[22] Dr. Harvey added that it will result in a greater understanding on the part of management of the need for joint discussions with employees representatives in advance of change.

Past experience with co-determination with one-third employee representation provides some insights into a possible reduction in tension. Twenty-eight executives of 21 European multinationals reacted to statement #4: "Co-determination resulted in a reduction of the atmosphere of distrust between labor and management," while 82 percent of the executives considered co-determination to have a positive impact on the relationship between labor and management. A vast 94 percent of the 17 interviewed workers' representatives agreed with this (see Table 8.5). In summary, it is the general consensus among executives and workers that the atmosphere of distrust between labor and management was significantly reduced as a result of co-determination. This reduction in distrust is important especially for multinational enterprises.

TABLE 8.5. Frequency of Responses to Statement 4.

	Executives		Worker Representatives	
	No.	%	No.	%
Strongly agree	5	17.8	8	47
Agree	18	64.3	8	47
Undecided	1	3.6	1	6
Disagree	4	14.3	0	0
Strongly Disagree	0	0	0	0
Total	28	100	17	100

Source: Compiled by the author.

Often, labor organizations and local governments look upon a multinational with distrust. A more opening up of the decision-making process may result in a more hospitable attitude toward the multinational corporation as employees will start to better understand the workings of this type of organization. Connected with this, the question arises: what are the specific effects of co-determination for U.S. multinationals operating with subsidiaries subject to co-determination? This topic will be discussed in Chapter 9.

CONCLUSION

Co-determination, as required by law in most West European countries, has implications for corporations, workers, shareholders, and society. Several of these implications have been discussed in this chapter.

European unions wish to concentrate power in their hands, creating a situation whereby the unions influence the total economic system of a country. Conflict of interest situations arise as a result of this union power, as union officers occupy seats on boards of competing companies and the unions may even own one or more of these competing companies.

Stalemates in decision making are possible as a result of the opposing interests of shareholders and workers. Experience with co-determination, as required in the coal, iron, and steel industries in West Germany, shows no evidence of this. Most decisions are screened and discussed in the works councils before bringing them before the supervisory board.

Workers have a positive attitude toward the co-determination concept in general. However, workers were found to be much more in favor of participation in decision making at the shopfloor level instead of at the corporate decision-making level. Secondly, the white collar workers are dissatisfied with co-determination as they are excluded from the decision-making processes.

Employers fear the effects of co-determination on the collective bargaining system. The latter works best when parties are of equal strength and independent of each other. Co-determination distorts these relationships and creates conflict of interests situations in the collective bargaining process.

The relaxing of tension between labor and management is a positive result of co-determination. The greater understanding on the part of management of the need for joint discussion with the employees' representatives in advance of the change is especially beneficial for the multinational enterprise, which often faces a high degree of distrust.

NOTES

1. For a complete description of the research methodology, see Chapter 1.
2. Dr. Geckler, Memorandum, Deutsche Gewerkschaft Bund, (Düsseldorf, 1965).

3. Wolfgang Heintzeler, "Is the American Board of the 1980's Now Being Tested in Europe?," Paper presented at the Corporate Director's Conference, Washington, D.C., December 1974, p. 1.

4. Gisbert Kley, *Replies to the DGB's Demands* (Köln: Bundesvereinigung der Deutschen Arbeitgeberverbände), p. 53.

5. For an excellent analysis of Loderer's power on the supervisory board of Volkswagen see: Alfred L. Thimm, "Decision Making at Volkswagen 1972–1975," *Columbia Journal of World Business* XI (Spring 1976):94–103; Paul Kemezis, "Keeping Labor Peace in Germany," *The New York Times*, April 11, 1976, p. 7.

6. See also: Robert J. Kühne, "Implications of Co-determination for the Insurance Industry," Paper presented at the American Risk and Insurance Association annual meeting, Scottsdale, Arizona, August 15, 1977.

7. From the author's interview with Mr. Vermeulen and Mr. R. Hoorens van Heijningen, Verbond van Nederlandse Ondernemingen (VNO), Den Haag, The Netherlands, August 1975.

8. From the author's interview with a spokesman of a major electronics company in West Germany, January 1977.

9. Confederation of German Employers' Associations, "Comments of the Confederation of German Employers' Associations on the Government Projects in the Field of Parity Co-determination and Asset Formation," unpublished paper, May 17, 1974, p. 3.

10. "Workers on the Board," *Forbes* (June 1, 1976) p. 67.

11. From the author's interview with Mr. Coleman, European Economic Community, August 1975, Brussels.

12. Gisbert Kley, op. cit., p. 35.

13. Wolfgang Heintzeler, op. cit., p. 1.

14. Sample size of the EMNID-Institut study is unknown. Several unsuccessful attempts were made to obtain this information.

15. From the author's interview with Mr. Haighton, Philips N.V., Eindhoven, The Netherlands, August 1975.

16. From the author's interview with Dr. Ivo A.A. van Haren, AKZO Nederland B.V., The Netherlands, August 1975.

17. From the author's interview with Dr. P.G. Harvey, Chairman, Mond Division, Imperial Chemical Industries, Ltd., August 1975, Runcorn, England.

18. Haighton, op. cit. (interview).

19. From the author's interview with Mr. H.J. De Bijll Nachenius, Unilever, Rotterdam, The Netherlands, August 1975.

20. Ivo van Haren, op. cit. (interview).

21. From the author's interview with Mr. Steins, worker-director on the board of management of Hoesch A.G., Dortmund, Germany, August 1975.

22. Dr. P.G. Harvey, op. cit. (interview).

9

IMPLICATIONS OF CO-DETERMINATION FOR U.S. MULTINATIONALS AND CONCLUSIONS

INTRODUCTION

It is possible that multinationals, such as Texaco, Exxon, Ford, Kodak, Mobil, General Motors, Goodyear, General Foods, IBM, International Harvestor, ITT, the 3M Company, and Proctor and Gamble, may lose control over their West German subsidiaries during the next few years. These and 20 other U.S. multinationals with subsidiaries in West Germany, employing roughly 200,000 people, are among the 650 companies subject to the West German Co-determination Act of 1976. Combined, these 650 companies account for about 80 percent of all production in West Germany.

The situation of these multinational corporations (MNC) in West Germany is not unique, as most European countries require some form of co-determination. Nearly all U.S. multinationals operate with one or more subsidiaries in some jurisdiction(s) that have mandatory co-determination. Existence of such requirements creates implications for the management and organization of multinational corporations. The objective here is to analyze these implications. Included are discussions of: (1) possible effect on future foreign investments, (2) position of U.S. multinationals in Europe, (3) effects upon the MNC headquarters' control over its wholly owned and joint venture subsidiaries, and (4) fear among MNC managers that the United States may require co-determination at some future date.

POSITION OF MULTINATIONAL CORPORATIONS IN EUROPE

There are no exceptions in the co-determination laws for foreign direct investments. Subsidiaries of MNCs are subject to the same requirements as domestic companies in the host country. Most countries do not allow exceptions for multinationals because of unions' pressure. Unions in Europe do not look favorably upon multinationals because foreign (particularly U.S.) enterprises often exclude themselves from the national labor relations systems.[1] Some U.S. multinationals, such as IBM, do not participate in local employers' associations. In addition, the International Chemical Federation accused Kodak of "antiunion" behavior.[2]

The unions in Europe fear the power of multinationals, as the latter have huge financial resources and can move production to other areas. Unions hope effective co-determination will decrease the power of multinationals. This is most likely to be realized when co-determination provides employees real participation in strategy formulation for the subsidiaries and decreased control from corporate headquarters.

Executives of U.S. multinationals with European subsidiaries are concerned. They protested against adoption of the new employees' participation law in West Germany, warning that there would be a negative impact on the 6.5 billion dollar U.S. investment in the country. How much real reduction in present and future investments will occur because of the new co-determination law is still difficult to estimate.

IMPLICATIONS FOR MULTINATIONALS' OPERATIONS

Multinationals with subsidiaries in Europe must adjust their structure and operations to adhere to the co-determination laws. The choice is limited. Either the organizational structure of the subsidiary is changed and adjusted to the co-determination laws of the host country or the multinational divests of the subsidiary. It is not expected that any U.S. multinationals will divest its European subsidiaries because of co-determination requirements. However, it is expected that they will take a cautious approach to any future investments in Western Europe.

Twelve executives of 12 different U.S. multinationals reacted to statement #1: "The new German Co-determination Act of 1976 will result in a reevaluation of future investments in West Germany." All were based in the United States. A full 75 percent stated that this reevaluation will take place (see Table 9.1).

Multinationals adjusting the structure of the decision-making boards of the subsidiary will face problems. Internally, the subsidiary faces problems such as implementation and adaptation, hostility of middle management, and disinterest among workers. Externally, it will have to cope with strong union power.[3] The relationship between multinationals' headquarters and subsidiaries may change. Loss of control may take place.

TABLE 9.1. Frequency of Responses to Statement 1.

	Executives of U.S. Multinationals	
	No.	%
Strongly agree	1	8.3
Agree	8	66.7
Undecided	0	0
Disagree	3	25
Strongly disagree	0	0
Total	12	100

Source: Compiled by the author.

Loss of Control

The co-determination laws result in employees and their unions obtaining a voice in the decision-making processes, and shareholders may lose much of their control over the company.[4] By giving up part of the managerial decision-making power to employees and unions, shareholders can lose control over their investments. That is, they stand to lose power now exercised through the general meeting. Multinationals, often the sole shareholder in their subsidiary, may lose control as well.

Twelve executives of 12 U.S. multinationals with subsidiaries in Europe, 28 executives of 21 European multinationals, and 16 German workers' or unions' representatives of 12 German companies responded to statement #2: "The German Co-determination Act of 1976, the British Bullock proposals, and the European Economic Community proposal will not alter the ownership relationship between the multinational's headquarters and its subsidiaries subject to any of the above laws." The statement met with disagreement from 85 percent of the executives, who felt that co-determination influences the ownership relationship. No significant difference was present in the opinions of West German versus U.S. executives.

Change in the ownership relationship was also expected by 75 percent of the workers' and unions' representatives. This answer was expected as the West German unions push for co-determination requirements to obtain change in the owners' control over their investment (see Table 9.2).

The supervisory board, on which the shareholders' representatives may no longer be in a majority because of co-determination, takes the initiative to hire and fire members of the board of management and decides on acquisitions, shutdowns, and so on. Shareholders' representatives may be deprived of the

TABLE 9.2. Frequency of Responses to Statement 2.

	Management		Workers' Representatives Unions	
	No.	%	No.	%
Strongly agree	0	0	0	0
Agree	2	5	2	12.5
Undecided	4	10	2	12.5
Disagree	24	60	9	56.25
Strongly agree	10	25	3	18.75
Total	40	100	16	100

Source: Compiled by the author.

freedom of decision based on the ownership of productive capital. The stockholders (or foreign investors) will keep the risk, but they will not control key factors influencing the degree of risk. Workers' representatives can exercise the traditional rights of ownership without bearing the customary accompanying responsibility.

No longer does full ownership mean full control. Shared control exists—shared control among stockholders and labor. The degree of shared control depends on the particular statutory co-determination requirements. Several examples can be cited whereby a loss of control can take place because of co-determination. Normally, in the international managerial decision-making process, the multinational's headquarters formulates the strategies and policies in the form of directions and advice, and these are coordinated in the local subsidiary. Loss of control brings on a situation in which the MNCs' headquarters issue directions to the subsidiary to be implemented but the subsidiary's supervisory board refuses to implement these directions. Day-to-day management of the local subsidiary depends upon decisions imposed upon it by the subsidiary's supervisory board. If the latter disagrees with directions received from headquarters, then it has the power to issue different orders.

A distinction can be made between two types of ownership of a multi-national's subsidiary: (1) full ownership, and (2) joint-venture. In either type, control can be lost. It is less likely that loss of control will occur with a full ownership position than with a joint venture.

In a wholly owned subsidiary subject to co-determination requirements, employees' representatives can obtain up to 50 percent of the seats on the supervisory board. In the case of parity co-determination, the owners cannot make any decisions without at least one supportive vote from among the employees' representatives. The law states that in case of a stalemate, the board chairman casts an additional vote to break the tie. The shareholders will keep control over the organization as long as the chairman is a shareholders' representative. The German Co-determination Act of 1976 states that the board chairman gets elected with a two-thirds majority vote by the supervisory board members. A provision is added that if this majority is not reached the shareholders' representatives will appoint the chairman, and the workers' representatives the vice-chairman.

The unions are opposed to this provision of electing the board chairman. They feel that workers are not participating in corporate decision making on an equal footing with the shareholders, as the chairman has the tie-breaking vote and can swing every decision in favor of the shareholders. Unions are, therefore, pressing for a change in the law. They want the chairman position to alternate yearly between a shareholders' representative and a workers' representative. Multinationals will lose control over their subsidiaries during the years that a workers' representative is chairman, as the labor-oriented chairman will have the tie-breaking vote. The multinational has full ownership but less than full control over its investment.

The multinational can get in a difficult position when it engages in a joint venture. Imagine a situation whereby an MNC and a local partner have 90 and ten percent ownership respectively and the subsidiary is subject to parity co-determination. Employees' representatives have 50 percent of the supervisory board seats, and the MNC and the local partner share the other 50 percent— 45 percent for the MNC and five percent for the local partner. It is conceivable that on some questions the local partner will vote for nationalistic or other reasons with the employees' representatives, for instance, in questions regarding repatriating profits or new investments. The local partner with his small percentage of ownership will often have a tie-breaking vote, and the MNC is dependent upon the partner's goodwill.

In 1979, most West European countries allowed employees to occupy one-third of the supervisory board seats. This means that if the MNC has full ownership, it also holds the remaining two-thirds of the seats and it, therefore, has full control over the subsidiary. Even in the case of a joint venture, it is possible to keep control, as long as the MNC holds 51 percent of the supervisory board seats. If employees have one-third of the seats and the MNC has 51 percent, then 15.66 percent remains for the local partner and the MNC keeps control.

The European Company Statute and the Bullock proposal both call for a three-way split on the supervisory board between shareholders' representatives, employees' representatives, and independent or general interests' representatives. In principle, these arrangements imply that the MNCs lose complete control over their subsidiaries, as stockholders will hold a minority position on the subsidiary's supervisory board. The stockholders will often be dependent upon the general interests' representatives to break the tie.

Several European countries are considering laws in which companies are annually required to distribute corporate shares to their employees. As shareholders, the workers are allowed to nominate shareholders' representatives to the board. These representatives are likely to be worker-oriented, as they are elected with support of the workers. Under co-determination, these worker-oriented representatives, combined with the statutory workers' representatives, will soon put the workers in a majority position on the board.

Loss of control has implications for management and organization of multinational corporations. Policies formulated at headquarters often depend upon the cooperation of all subsidiaries. One single dysfunction can jeopardize total operations of the MNC and implementation of the policy. Boundaries are placed around the discretion of the multinational's headquarters, which may be deprived of the freedom of decision based on the ownership of productive capital. Decisions, even those affecting the interests of employees, may not always be made with regard to the principles of economics.

The experience of the Dutch multinational AKZO N.V. is an example of a multinational losing control over its subsidiaries. For economic reasons, AKZO N.V. wanted to cut down the operations of its Enka Glanzstoff division all over Europe. Enka Glanzstoff, which is organized on a geographic basis, is in the fibers industry. Enka Glanzstoff's operations in each country are supervised by the local subsidiary of AKZO N.V., for instance in Holland, through AKZO-Nederland B.V.

During Enka Glanzstoff's reorganization, the holding company (AKZO N.V.) ran into noncooperative local subsidiaries. Several supervisory boards of subsidiaries operating in countries with statutory co-determination refused to execute AKZO N.V.'s order. They decided only to cooperate with AKZO N.V.'s decision if the latter would provide expensive layoff plans for the workers. The layoff plans and daily financial losses in the Enka Glanzstoff division were a big drain on AKZO N.V.'s reserves. Operations were finally curtailed and workers layed off. AKZO N.V. was saved from being the first multinational to go bankrupt as a result of co-determination requirements.

CO-DETERMINATION IN THE UNITED STATES?

Executives of U.S. multinationals protest against the adoption of co-determination legislation in Western Europe. The protests are based on two major reasons: first, protection of investments (as analyzed in the previous section), and secondly, a fear that U.S. unions and workers might start demanding co-determination rights.

The purpose of this section is to analyze the possible effects of co-determination on the U.S. industrial democracy and to speculate as to whether or not co-determination is coming to the United States. Included are analyses of the current differences between the organization of unions and union movement in Western European countries and the United States and an evaluation of the opinions and standpoints by U.S. labor leaders, management, and government officials.[5]

United States versus European Labor Movements

There are significant differences between the organization of unions and labor movements of Europe and the United States. Unions in Western European countries are set up along broad industrial lines and are not centered around individual enterprises. In West Germany, for instance, there are 16 trade unions, and each union represents all workers in a given industry. These 16 unions are grouped into one trade union confederation, the *Deutsche Gewerkschaftsbund* (DGB). Each union controls a large number of workers and is strictly controlled from the top national level.

U.S. unions are not as well organized. The largest federation of unions in the United States is the AFL-CIO, which has over 130 national unions compared to the 16 of the DGB. This large number of unions, each with its own divergent interests, makes it extremely difficult to decide upon unified national goals.

The macro-oriented European bargaining structure, with industry-wide bargaining between employers' associations and national unions or even economy-wide bargaining between central federations of employers' associations and trade union federations, distinguishes itself from the micro-oriented U.S. bargaining structure with the individual enterprise-centered negotiations. However, it should be added that some U.S. companies involved in enterprise-centered negotiations, such as General Motors, are almost as large as some European countries such as Belgium, Holland, or Denmark.

The strong national union organization in most European countries, combined with the macro-oriented bargaining structure, provides unions with considerable influence in the national governments. In 1973, more than 240 members of the German parliament were also union members.[6] European unions, in contrast to U.S. unions, have close contact with political parties, and the latter often back, or are even dominated by, the unions. European labor unions have adopted political ideologies ranging in various degrees from mild socialism, as in the United Kingdom, to communism, as in Italy and France.

This close relationship between political parties and unions is not found in the United States. After the 1958 congressional elections, labor officials were confident of their positions because a large number of prolabor legislators had been elected. However, the labor unions had no universal definite goals. As a result, even with a majority of legislators being sympathetic to the causes of workers, the unions could not get any significant legislation beneficial to labor passed.[7] Another instance occurred in early 1977 when labor could not obtain the passage of the Common Situs Picketing Act or the repeal of section 14.b of the Taft–Hartley Act, dealing with right to work laws, even though both houses of Congress had Democratic majorities and a Democratic president was in office.

The goal of the European unions is a restructuring of the entire society on behalf of all workers,[8] based on mass organization and workers' solidarity. The percentage of union membership in Europe typically runs at 50 percent, as in the United Kingdom, and up to almost 90 percent in Sweden, whereas in the United States a little under one-third of the wage and salary force is organized. European workers are class conscious and organized in political parties, whereas U.S. workers are mainly concerned with their own individual interests.

There are other philosophical differences between the U.S. and the European labor movements. U.S. unions see themselves as a countervailing power to management, and they feel that the clear dividing line between trade unions' and management's functions must be maintained, since a trade union directly involved in management decisions would no longer be in a position to effectively define workers' interests. European unions feel that workers' interests are best protected by obtaining a direct say in corporate management decisions such as investments, production planning, layoffs, and so on. Instead of being a countervailing power to management, European unions wish to be a part of it.

Opinions

The opinions of union leaders are important when discussing a topic so closely related to labor. As shown in many European countries, the unions can successfully press for a change in law. Therefore, statements on this topic from Charles Levinson, secretary-general of the International Federation of Chemical and General Workers' Unions (ICF), with 4 million members, and representatives of both the AFL-CIO and the United Automobile Workers (UAW) union are included.

In his book *Industry's Democratic Revolution,* Charles Levinson states, while describing workers' participation:

> It is not being excessively optimistic to predict that within a decade the movement will expand with equal speed to certain countries in Latin America, Africa and Asia and will be seriously demanded by a number of the major unions in North America as well.[9]

Levinson, considered one of the major promoters of multinational unions, strongly favors co-determination. As the first step toward participatory management, Levinson expects an extension and widening of collective bargaining procedures, where the contents of the agreements will extend over many aspects of managerial prerogatives and decision-making power and confer much of the substance, if not the forms, developed in Europe.

U.S. union leaders have maintained a firm ideological attachment to collective bargaining.[10] They do not wish to break down the countervailing power position between labor and management, and they fear that co-determination will result in a conflict of interests or even confusion of functions. Thomas H. Donahue, executive assistant to the president of the AFL-CIO, explained in May 1976:

> We do not seek to be a partner in management—to be, most likely, the junior partner in success and the senior partner in failure. We do not want to blur in any way the distinctions between the respective roles in management and labor in the plant. We guard our independence fiercely—independent of government, independent of any political party and independent of management.[11]

Donahue expressed the AFL-CIO's wish not to break down the adversary relationship between labor and management and the confederation's desire for individualism.

George Meany, president of the AFL-CIO, stated in 1976, "It (co-determination) will not work here. The Germans did it because they were worried about someone like Hitler reappearing. But I never saw a union that was worth a damn unless it was free—complete and absolutely free."[12] The AFL-CIO has no official policy on participatory management or co-determination, and they seriously doubt whether American management and American labor are ready for this concept, let alone the public.

> A fundamental problem with the concept of co-determination in the United States is that it seems unlikely that management is willing to surrender any part of its decision making rights, unless the firm is in trouble. Thus, even if labor supported the concept, the only way we would be able to obtain it would be through legislation. I further doubt that there is support for the concept in government. In fact, it seems to me that it would require legislation today just to make it a mandatory issue of bargaining.[13]

The AFL-CIO's stand toward co-determination might change in the future as a result of considerable changes in the members of the AFL-CIO's executive council during 1977. Only on one known occasion did an AFL-CIO union propose co-determination. The International Federation of Professional and Technical Engineers, Local 81, AFL-CIO submitted a proposal during the 1976 annual meeting of American Telephone and Telegraph Company (A.T. and T.) "that the board of directors consider taking appropriate steps in future years to broaden its composition by nominating as proposed Directors representatives of employee labor organizations."[14] The directors of this nation's largest private employer, with nearly 1 million people on the payroll, A.T. and T. recommended a vote against the unions proposal.[15] It was turned down by 96.7 percent of the shares voted.[16]

Leonard Woodcock, former president of the nearly 1.5 million-member UAW, was one of the few U.S. union leaders in favor of co-determination, and he sees it as a humane approach to labor–management conflicts. Unsuccessful demands for two union officials as workers' representatives on the board of directors were included in the collective bargaining negotiation with Chrysler in July 1976. This demand was the result of Chrysler's offer to name British workers to Chrysler's 15-member U.K. board of directors, whose offer was turned down by the British unions. However, the UAW considered it a good idea and Douglas Fraser, UAW vice-president in charge of the union's Chrysler department, feels that, "One or two unionists on the (Chrysler) board could save it from the kind of blunders that almost sank it in 1974–75."[17]

Unions are becoming more and more aware that their members' attitudes are changing and that they underestimated the interest in workers' participation in the decisions at the work place. UAW's former president Leonard Woodcock described the future as follows:

> In coming years, workers of the new generation will inevitably seek a participatory role in all areas of decision making, not out of some ideological compulsion to destroy the "system" but out of a pragmatic interest in protecting themselves and their families from the multiple insecurities and inequities the current governance of the system breeds. The younger workers, as the U.S. Department of Labor has acknowledged in a profile of the American labor force in the 1970's, will be more insistent than their elders on having a continuing voice in matters that affect their jobs, their income and their environment.
>
> In other words, management can look forward to a further erosion of its self-arrogated, arbitrary and non-negotiable right throughout a whole range of decision making hitherto beyond the reach of collective bargaining. Not only will collective bargaining be pressed in new areas, it will be pressed not to give workers relief from the consequences of management's unilateral decisions, but rather to share in the decisions for the purpose of preventing the adverse consequences.
>
> Such joint decision-making will not be limited to the job and what might be called its management. It will extend to such matters, all of consequence to working people, as the removal of work from bargaining units, the closing and location of plants, and at least the right of consultation in such matters affecting workers as price, production and investment decision.[18]

Woodcock's expectations with respect to the contents of joint decision making in the near future run parallel to the types of decisions, such as closing and location of plants and possible investments, as discussed in European supervisory boards subject to co-determination. The degree to which workers will be allowed to participate in joint decision making may be different from Europe, but the content of the topics is the same.

Co-determination has received little government response outside Europe. Among U.S. legislators, Senator Jacob K. Javits (Republican, New York) felt that although co-determination has not been a complete success, "an effort to open up corporate board room opportunities to workers should have a salutory effect on improving the employees' appreciation for management problems as well as exposing management to workers' ideas."[19]

Only a few top level U.S. executives have experience with co-determination through the multinational's European subsidiaries. They are particularly worried about Germany's commitment to parity co-determination. Henry Ford went to West Germany to deliver the message that Ford does not want workers and unions moving into their boardrooms. General Motors fears employees' participation as well: "If German workers get to elect half of the board of an American company, General Motors fears that the United Automobile Workers Union in America might decide that it is a good idea in Detroit, too."[20] Chrysler's experience showed that this fear is justified and that the seed has been planted.

The majority of the interviewed executives of U.S. multinationals with subsidiaries in Europe is out their experiences with co-determination. They perceive the implications of co-determination to be detrimental for their operations, but at the same time the majority states that none of the supervisory boards of their European subsidiaries have made strategic decisions which would not have been made by a supervisory board without employees' representatives (see Tables 9.3, Question 1 and 9.4, Statement 3). Two-thirds of the interviewed U.S. executives perceived co-determination to be detrimental to their operations. Reasons for this may be the often negative press in

TABLE 9.3. Frequency of Responses to Question 1.

	U.S. Executives	
	No.	%
Very favorable	0	0
Favorable	4	13.3
Neutral	2	6.7
Detrimental	17	56.7
Very detrimental	3	10
Do not know	4	13.3
Total	30	100

Source: Compiled by the author.

TABLE 9.4. Frequency of Responses to Statement 3.

	U.S. Executives	
	No.	%
Strongly agree	0	0
Agree	9	30
Undecided	3	10
Disagree	18	60
Strongly disagree	0	0
Total	30	100

Source: Compiled by the author.

U.S. business publications related to co-determination and fear for workers' participation demands spreading in the United States.

The executives' perceptions are contradicted in their responses to a statement analyzing the influence of co-determination on strategic decision making. The same executives provided the answers in Tables 9.3 and 9.4. Most executives mentioned that the workers' representatives on the board have influenced the strategic decision making but that the final decision was not significantly different from the decision which would have been made by a supervisory board without employees' representatives. The reason for this may be that workers' representatives have not yet had a majority or equal voting power on a supervisory board anywhere.[21]

Analysis

Most managers of U.S. corporations try to ignore the existence of co-determination, mainly because they fear demands for similar participation rights in the United States. A personnel executive of the international division of a large U.S. pharmaceuticals company gave his personal view of the present situation: "It is ridiculous to preserve a certain style of management in the United States and to ignore things that are happening around the world, such as workers' participation, which change the old-fashioned management philosophy. The U.S. organizational structure should be considered obsolete."[22]

This executive continued to outline his company's philosophy toward workers' participation:

1. We are not supporters of co-determination defined to mean appointment of workers' representatives to a company's board of directors or any such similar

arrangement requiring comanagement of the business, however we will obey the law.

2. We generally do not invite or encourage the formation of works' councils in those countries in which there is no legal requirement to the formation of such councils. In countries in which works' councils are required by law it is important that they are used in management's best interest. Our training concentrates on that.

3. We should prevent workers' participation or works' councils, unless legally required to accept these, to be involved in those matters that are clearly management prerogatives such as marketing, management relocation, strategy formulation, finance, etc.[23]

Even though this company is not ignoring the existence of workers' participation, many others officially do. This does not mean that internally some U.S. corporations are not adapting to industrial relations changes or are studying workers' participation.

Five years ago General Motors was stressing cost effectiveness and productivity. Last year it was the quality of life and dignity of the worker, based on the idea that a successful worker will be a more productive worker.

To prepare themselves for possible future co-determination demands in the United States and to better adjust to contemporary co-determination laws in Europe, some U.S. corporations study workers' participation. These companies were found to be involved in three areas:

1. Someone in the personnel department studies mandatory workers' participation in detail and considers applications within the law which will enable local managers to utilize workers' participation as a management tool and as a means to increase workers' satisfaction, resulting in better productivity, profits, and overall business investment.

2. Appropriate managers, workers, and industrial relations personnel are trained in the development of administration and overall conduct guidelines of mandatory works' councils and other forms of workers' participation (this is based on the idea that if a company is subject to statutory requirements it may as well make sure that it capitalizes on workers' participation and does not work against it).

3. Research is being conducted into ways and means of resolving labor management problems both within and outside the traditional collective bargaining process to use mandatory workers' participation as an advantage to the corporation.[24]

The above discussion and examples outline the position taken by a small number of U.S. corporations, whereas it should be noted that these are the exception and that most U.S. companies ignore workers' participation. However, whatever stand the corporations take has limited significant bearing upon the possible future demands among U.S. workers and unions for co-determination.

The social, economic, and industrial relations conditions in which co-determination developed in Europe are significantly different from those in the United States. These differences have an impact upon possible demands among U.S. workers and unions for co-determination.

The European unions, because of the macro-oriented collective bargaining and close contacts with labor-oriented or labor-dominated political parties, can push for co-determination legislation through political channels. U.S. unions do not have such strong ties.

U.S. workers have no interest in co-determination because only a few are aware of it, and the U.S. work force is primarily based upon individualism. The latter explains why U.S. unions are exclusive in nature, trying to achieve as much as possible for their individual members instead of cooperating with other unions to achieve common goals such as co-determination. Because of the class consciousness of the European working people, unions there depend upon worker solidarity and mass organization, making it necessary for unions to cooperate with other unions to achieve common goals.

Co-determination requires that workers and unions work together with management in corporate decision making. The unions in Europe wish to be part of the management. U.S. unions, in contrast, see themselves as a countervailing power to management and wish to limit their activities to bargaining in labor and contract negotiations. The British unions, while pushing for the Bullock proposal, are in a transition period from an adversary relationship with management to one of cooperation with management. It will be of interest to study this transition as it may one day influence a possible change in relationship between unions and management in the United States.

Co-determination provides workers with a voice in decisions about plant closures and relocations, large investments, and redistribution of works. Employees' representatives on the supervisory board can also influence decisions such as financing, selling, marketing, and the selection of the board of management. There is a limited interest among U.S. unions and workers to influence decisions that are not job related, such as financing and marketing, but unions do wish to be included in discussions about plant shutdowns, relocations, and new investments.

In summary, co-determination should not be expected in the next few years in the United States for the earlier outlined reasons (including workers' apathy and unions' unwillingness to give up its countervailing power position toward management. Unions wishing to be included in discussions about plant shutdowns, relocations, and new investments must do so at first through an extension of the concept of collective bargaining. This is not identical to allowing employees' representatives on the board of directors, but the extended concept of collective bargaining will have the same effects as co-determination, as all significant managerial decisions affecting labor will be influenced by labor. The next step will be demands for workers or their representatives on the board of directors. In this matter, co-determination demands should be expected in the United States before 1990, probably first negotiated in a contract in one individual company or industry and later extended to all companies.

CONCLUSIONS

Managers of organizations engaged in international business often realize that they face a more variate spectrum of constraints and contingencies than their domestic counterparts. The manager of the domestic operations faces one single economic system, one labor relations system, and so on. As business becomes more international, it is increasingly important to understand political and business climates in other countries. Legislation in one or more foreign countries can jeopardize the total worldwide operations of a multinational.

The manager of the multinational corporation should be flexible and must be able to understand and cope with a multitude of economic, legal, and labor relations systems because each country in which the multinational operates has its own particular legal requirements. An example is the statutory co-determination requirements in several West European countries. All countries with co-determination have different types of requirements. This, combined with increasing demands for co-determination in many areas around the world, provides labor relations managers with a difficult task in analyzing all the different requirements pertaining to co-determination, and its possible effects.

The implications of co-determination as they affect the operations of MNCs should be analyzed. The co-determination legislation results in a power concentration in the hands of the trade unions, and the latter influences the total economic system of a country, creating an economy centrally controlled by the trade unions. Conflict of interest situations arise because: (1) officials of the same union can occupy seats on supervisory boards of competing companies, and (2) unions own large corporations themselves, which compete with companies that may have a union representative on its board.

It is often assumed that workers in Europe are satisfied with co-determination and that they are really interested. This author's survey revealed that German workers are not really interested in co-determination. Workers are disappointed with the effects of co-determination and do not include it on a list of immediate interests. They were found to be more interested in participating in decision making at the shopfloor level, and they have a positive attitude toward works councils. Workers consider the latter a much better vehicle for communications. Therefore, it was suggested that if a desire for participatory management exists, this should be implemented at the shopfloor level of the organization instead of starting immediately at the policy-formulating level of the organization.

White collar workers strongly oppose co-determination as they are by-passed in most co-determination models and they often do not belong to a union. The latter consider them a threat to the union's struggle for power. As a result, white collar workers are organizing in separate unions to protect their interests. Exclusion of white collar workers from co-determination makes the latter unjustifiable in industries with a high percentage of white collar workers and a low degree of unionization.

A significant advantage of co-determination for multinationals is the relaxing of tension between labor and management. A reduction of distrust between local nationals and the multinational could result from co-determination. A greater understanding on the part of management of the need for joint discussions with the employees' representatives in advance of change will be a positive effect of co-determination on the multinational's operations.

No exceptions in the co-determination requirements are made for foreign direct investors. European unions pressured local governments to include both domestic- and foreign-owned corporations under the legislation. The co-determination laws require the headquarters of U.S. multinationals operating with subsidiaries in Western Europe to restructure the subsidiary at the corporate decision-making level to satisfy the requirements.

A reduction in the headquarters control and influence over the decision-making processes and determination of the corporate policies and strategies takes place as a result of co-determination. There is now a situation of shared control—shared between the representatives of stockholders and employees. On the supervisory board, the possible opposing interests of stockholders and workers face each other, resulting in a decrease in the efficiency of decision making.

The degree to which multinationals lose control depends upon (1) the percentage of supervisory board seats designated for workers' representatives, and (2) the type of ownership. In a wholly owned subsidiary it is less likely that a loss of control takes place, as opposed to a joint venture, whereby a local partner may vote with the employees for nationalistic or other reasons. This loss of control affects the total operations of the multinational as the operations of one subsidiary normally have an impact upon the operations of the MNC's other subsidiaries.

Co-determination has become a reality for most U.S. multinational enterprises operating with subsidiaries in Europe, and most U.S. managers officially deplore co-determination, not because of significant negative experience with co-determination but because they fear that U.S. unions might demand the same rights as their European counterparts. U.S. multinationals try to ignore co-determination, hoping that it will not become a reality in the

United States, and almost all U.S. unions have little or no interest in co-determination per se. However, unions wish to extend the concept of collective bargaining to include decisions related to layoffs, plant shutdowns, relocations, and new investments. It has been suggested that co-determination demands should be expected in the United States before 1990, probably first as an extension of the collective bargaining process.

NOTES

1. W. Albeda, "Multinationals en arbeidsverhoudingen," *tvvs*, 18 (January 1975):19.
2. Ibid., p. 21.
3. These problems were discussed in Chapter 8.
4. Part of this section is from: Robert J. Kühne, "Co-determination: Mutiny on the Multinational?," in *Proceedings* (The Academy of International Business, 1977), pp. 123–25.
5. Part of this selection is from: Robert J. Kühne, "Co-determination in the United States?: An Analysis," in *Management in an Age of Complexity and Change*, ed. Dennis F. Ray and Thad B. Green (Mississippi State University, Mississippi: 1977), pp. 72–74. See also William Cowie, "Is Co-determination Likely in America?" unpublished paper.
6. Frank Vogl, *German Business After the Economic Miracle* (New York: Halsted Press, 1973), p. 75.
7. Neil W. Chamberlain and Donald E. Cullen, *The Labor Sector* (New York: McGraw Hill, 1971), p. 451.
8. Everett H. Kassalow, *Trade Unions and Industrial Relations on International Comparison* (New York: Random House, 1969), p. 14.
9. Charles Levinson, *Industry's Democratic Revolution* (London: Allen and Unwin, 1974), p. 73.
10. Milton Derber, "Collective Bargaining," *The Annals* 431 (May 1977):92.
11. Ibid., p. 92.
12. "Workers on the Board," *Forbes* 117 (June 1, 1976):66.
13. Letter to the author from John L. Zalusky, economist, Research Department, on behalf of George Meany, President of the AFL-CIO, explaining some opinions of the AFL-CIO, January 29, 1976.
14. "Notice of 1976 Annual Meeting and Proxy Statement," (New York: American Telephone and Telegraph Company, 1976), p. 16.
15. Ibid., p. 17.
16. "1976 Annual Meeting of Share Owners," (New York: American Telephone and Telegraph Company, 1976), p. 21.
17. See: Neil McInnes, "People's Capitalism," *Barron's* 56 (July 12, 1976):9.
18. Leonard Woodcock, "U.S.A.," in *Industry's Democratic Revolution*, ed. Charles Levinson (London: Allen and Unwin, 1974), p. 216.
19. German Information Center, "Co-determination," unpublished paper (1974), p. 2.
20. "American Multinationals Want to Go Home," *The Economist* 259 (April 17, 1976):85–86.
21. There is no experience yet with the German Co-determination Act of 1976, which is still in the implementation stage.
22. From the author's interview with a personnel executive of the international division of a large U.S. pharmaceuticals company, March 1979.
23. Ibid.
24. These three areas were suggested by Mr. Reyer Swaak, director of personnel, Schering Corporation, Kenilworth, New Jersey.

BIBLIOGRAPHY

Agthe, Klaus E. "Mitbestimmung: Report on a Social Experiment." *Business Horizons* 20 (February 1977): 5–14.

Aguren, Stefan, et al. *The Volvo Kalmar Plant, The Impact of New Design on Work Organization.* Stockholm, Sweden: The Rationalization Council SAF-LO, Box 16120, S-10323, 1976.

Albeda, W. "Multinationals en arbeidsverhoudingen." *tvvs* 18 (January 1975): 18–22.

Alutto, J. and Acito, F. "Decisional Participation and Sources of Job Satisfaction: A Study of Manufacturing Personnel." *Academy of Management Journal* 17 (June 1974): 339–47.

"American Multinationals Want to Go Home." *The Economist* 259 (April 17, 1976): 85–6.

Arbeitskreises Mitbestimmung. *Stellungnahme des Arbeitskreises Mitbestimmung zum Mitbestimmungsgesetz* (Köln: Bundesvereinigung der Deutschen Arbeitgeberverbände, 1976).

Armstrong, J. Scott. "Social Irresponsibility in Management." *Journal of Business Research* 5 (September 1977): 185–213.

Aspengren, Tor. "Norway." In *Industry's Democratic Revolution*, edited by Charles Levinson, pp. 219–30. London: Allen and Unwin, 1974.

Balke, Siegfried. *Creeping Syndicalism by Participation?* Köln: Bundesvereinigung der Deutschen Arbeitgeberverbände, 1968.

Bertsch, Gary K. and Ganschow, Thomas W. *Comparative Communism: The Soviet Chinese and Yugoslav Models.* San Francisco: W.H. Freeman, 1976.

Biedenkopf, K.H. *Mitbestimmung im Unternehmen.* Deutscher Bundestag, 6, Wahlperiode, VI/334, 1970.

Blumberg, Phillip I. "From the Boardroom: Implications of Representation Trend for U.S. Corporations." *Harvard Business Review* 55 (January–February 1977): 45–53.

Boonzaijer, Flaes, R.M. "Arbeiderscontrole in Joegoslavie." *Intermediair* 11 (August 15, 1975): 11–15.

Bragge, J.E. and Andrews, I.R. "Participative Decision-Making: An Experimental Study in a Hospital." *Journal of Applied Behavioral Science* 9 (1973): 727–35.

Brown, Courtney C. *Putting the Corporate Board to Work.* New York: Macmillan Publishing Co. Inc., 1976.

Bundesvereinigung der Deutschen Arbeitgeberverbände. *Das neue Betriebsverfassungsgesetz.* Köln: Bundesvereinigung der Deutschen Arbeitgeberverbände, 1972.

Carlson, Elliot. "Participation Yugoslavian Style." *International Management* 28 (April 1973): 74–82.

Carlson, Harry. "Joint Industrial Councils in Great Britain." *Monthly Labor Review* 48 (May 1939): 1046–54.

Carson, Iain. "Preparing Workers for Participation." *International Management* 28 (January 1973): 44–5.

Chamberlain, Neil W. and Cullen, Donald E. *The Labor Sector.* New York: McGraw Hill, 1971.

Clutterbuch, David. "How Effective are Worker Directors?" *International Management* 29 (February 1974): 15–6.

Coch, L. and French, J. "Overcoming Resistance to Change." *Human Relations* 1 (1948): 512–32.
"Co-determination: When Workers Help Manage." *Business Week* (July 14, 1975): 133–34.

Coleman, X.X. Assistant to the European Commission Commissioner for Internal Market Affairs, Brussels, Belgium. Interview, August 12, 1975.

Commission of the European Communities. *Employee Participation and Company Structure.* Brussels: European Communities, 1975.

Confederation of German Employers' Associations. "Comments of the Confederation of German Employers' Associations on the Government Projects in the Field of Parity Co-Determination and Asset Formation." unpublished paper, May 17, 1974.

Cooper, Michael R. and Wood, Michael. "Effects of Member Participation and Commitment in Group Decision Making on Influence, Satisfaction and Decision Riskiness." *Journal of Applied Psychology* 59 (April 1974): 127–34.

Copeland, Melvin T., and Towl, Andrew R. *The Board of Directors and Business Management.* Andover, Massachusetts: The Andover Press, 1974.

Crane, Donald P. "The Case for Participative Management." *Business Horizons* 19 (April 1976): 15–21.

Davenport, Russell. "Enterprise for Everyman." *Fortune* XLI (January 1950): 50–8.

De Bijil Nachenius, H.J. Nederlandse Unilever-bedrijven, B.V., Rotterdam, The Netherlands. Interview, August 1975.

Delperee, A. "Joint Committees in Belgium." *International Labour Review* 81 (March 1960): 185–204.

De Man, Henry. "Industrial Councils in Belgium." *Survey* 44 (July 3, 1920): 478–82.

Denitch, Bogdan. "The Relevance of Yugoslav Self-Management." In *Comparative Communism*, edited by Gary K. Bertsch and Thomas W. Ganschow, pp. 268–81. San Francisco: W.H. Freeman, 1976.

Derber, Milton. "Collective Bargaining." *The Annals* 431 (May 1977): 83–94.

_____. "Crosscurrents in Worker Participation." *Industrial Relations* 9 (February 1970): 123–36.

_____. "The Idea of Industrial Democracy in America: 1915–1935." *Labor History* 8 (Winter 1967): 3–29.

Descamps, Eugene, "France." In *Industry's Democratic Revolution,* edited by Charles Levinson, pp. 120–152. London: Allen and Unwin, 1974.

"De verzwegen Nipo-enquête." *Elsevier Magazine* (February 7, 1976): 14–15.

Drion, T. "De herbouw van ons ondernemingsrecht." *Op Eigen Terrein,* Unilever N.V., Rotterdam, March 2, March 16 and April 13, 1972.

Drucker, Peter F. "The Battle Over Co-Determination." *The Wall Street Journal* 190 (August 10, 1977): 14.

"Establishment of Works Committees in Italy." *International Labour Review* 57 (January 1948): 72–5.

European Communities. *The Facts.* Brussels: Commission of the European Communities, June 1972.

European Economic Community. *Employee Participation and Community Structure.* Brussels: Commission of the European Communities, Supplement 8 of 1975.

Fawcett, Edmund. "European Companies." *European Community* (July–August 1975): 3–7.

Fisher, Paul. "Labor Co-determination in Germany." *Social Research* 18 (December 1951): 477.

Flaes, R.M. Boonzaijer. "Arbeiderscontrole in Joegoslavie." *Intermediair* 11 (August 15, 1975): 11–15.

Foy, Nancy and Herman Gadon. "Worker Participation: Contrasts in Three Countries." *Harvard Business Review* 54 (May–June 1976): 73–8.

French, C.E. "The Shop Committee in the U.S." *Johns Hopkins University Studies in Historical and Political Science* 51 (1923): 9–105.

French, J. "An Experiment on Participation in a Norwegian Factory." *Human Relations* 13 (1960): 3–19.

French, J., E. Kay, and H.H. Meyer. "Participation and the Appraisal System." *Human Relations* 19 (1966): 3–19.

Frost, Carl F., John H. Wakeley and Robert A. Ruh. *The Scanlon Plan for Organization Development: Identity, Participation and Equity.* East Lansing, Michigan: Michigan State University Press, 1974.

Fürstenburg, Friedrich. "West German Experience with Industrial Democracy." *The Annals* 431 (May 1977): 44–53.

Geckler, Dr. *Memorandum.* Düsseldorf: DGB, Niedersachsen, 1965.

Geijer, Arne. "Sweden." In *Industry's Democratic Revolution,* edited by Charles Levison, pp. 268–79. London: Allen and Unwin, 1974.

German Information Center. "Co-determination, A Survey of the Bill on Employee Participation in Management Decision Making." Unpublished paper, October 1974.

Gray, Edmund R. and C. Ray Gullett. *Employee Representation at Standard Oil Company of New Jersey, A Case Study.* Baton Rouge: Louisiana State University, 1973.

Green, William. "The Challenge of the Union." *American Federationist* 32 (March 1925): 161–64.

Greiner, Larry E. "What Managers Think of Participative Leadership." *Harvard Business Review* 51 (March–April 1973): 111–17.

Haighton, Mr. Philips, N.V. Eindhoven, The Netherlands. Interview. August 1975.

Hans-Böckler-Gesellschaft e.V. "Das Mitbestimmungsgesprach." *Gewerkschaftliche Monatshefte* (October–November–December 1973): 216–22.

Hartmann, Heinz. "Co-determination Today and Tomorrow." *British Journal of Industrial Relations* 13 (March 1975): 54–9.

Harvey, P.G. Chairman, Mond Division, ICI, England. Interview, August 1975.

_____. "Communication and Participation." HRH The Duke of Edinburgh's Study Conference: Industry in Society, Oxford, 5–20 July 1974. Conference Paper No. 10.

Heintzeler, Wolfgang. "Is the American Board of the 1980's Now Being Tested in Europe?" Corporate Directors' Conference. Presentation Washington, D.C., December 17, 1974.

Herschel, Wilhelm. "Employee Representation in the Federal Republic of Germany." *International Labour Review* 64 (August–September 1955): 207–15.

Holter, Harriet. "Attitudes Towards Employee Participation in Company Decision Making." *Human Relations* 18 (1965): 297–321.

Hrdlitschka, Wilhelm. "Austria." In *Industry's Democratic Revolution*, ed. Charles Levinson, pp. 280–300. London: Allen and Unwin, 1974.

Hromadka, Wolfgang. *Betriebsverfassungsgesetz* 1972. München: Institut Mensch und Arbeit, 1972.

"Industrial Democracy has its Snags." *The Economist* 241 (March 9, 1974): 74.

Informationsdienst des Instituts der Deutschen Wirtschaft. "Der Entwurf des neuen Mitbes-timmungsgesetzes." *IWD Newsletter* 2, No. 12 (March 18, 1976): 4–6.

Institut der deutschen Wirtschaft. "Mitbestimmung." *Argumente zu Unternehmerfragen.* Köln: Deutscher Instituts-Verlag, 1976.

"International Outlook." *Business Week* (June 6, 1977): 49.

Jerovsek, Janez. "Self-Management-System in Yugoslav Enterprises." *Industrial Relations* 15 (February 1975): 113–22.

"Joint Committees in Belgium." *International Labour Review* 53 (January–February 1946): 81–2.

"Joint Labour-Management Committees in the United States." *International Labour Review* 45 (May 1942): 554.

"Joint Production Committees." *International Labour Review* 50 (December 1944): 775–76.

"Joint Production Committees for Royal Ordnance Factories in Great Britain." *International Labour Review* 45 (May 1942): 552–54.

"Joint Production Committees in Norway." *International Labour Review* 53 (March–April 1946): 222–24.

"Joint Production Committees in the French Aircraft Industry." *International Labour Review* 50 (September, 1944): 364–65.

Judith, Rudolph. *Text zur Mitbestimmung.* Industriegewerkshaft Metall, undated.

Kassalow, Everett. *Trade Unions and Industrial Relations on International Comparison.* New York: Random House, 1969.

Kerr, Clark. "The Trade Union Movement and the Redistribution of Power in Postwar Germany." *The Quarterly Journal of Economics* 68 (November 1954): 535–64.

Kemezis, Paul. "Keeping Labor Peace in Germany." *The New York Times*, April 11, 1976, p. 7.

Kley, Gisbert. "Replies to the DGB's Demands." Köln: Bundesvereinigung der Deutschen Arbeitgeberverbände, undated.

Koontz, Harold. *The Board of Directors and Effective Management.* New York: McGraw-Hill, 1967.

Krishan, R. "Democratic Participation in Decision Making by Employees in American Corporations." *Academy of Management Journal* 17 (June 1974): 339–47.

Kühne, Robert J. "Co-determination in the United States? An Analysis." In *Management in an Age of Complexity and Change*, edited by Dennis F. Ray and Thad B. Green, pp. 72–4. Mississippi State, Mississippi: Southern Management Association, 1977.

_____. "Statutory Co-determination: Mutiny on the Multinational?" *1977 Proceedings*, Miami, Florida: Academy of International Business, pp. 123–25.

_____. "Implications of Co-determination for the Insurance Industry." Annual National Meeting of the American Risk and Insurance Association, Scottsdale, Arizona. Presentation, August 1977.

_____. "Legal Requirements for the American Board of Directors in 1985, Now Being Tested in Europe." Annual National Meeting of the Academy of Management, Kansas City, Kansas. Presentation, August 1976.

_____. "Management Problems for International Enterprises Operating in Nations with Statutory Co-Determination at the Board Level." Annual National Meeting of the Academy of Management, Kansas City, Kansas. Presentation, August 1976.

_____. "Co-determination: A Statutory Re-Structuring of the Organization." *Columbia Journal of World Business* 11 (Summer 1976): 17–25.

Kühne, Robert J. and Smith, David M. "Worker Participation in Europe: A Historical Overview." Annual National Meeting of the Academy of Management, Orlando, Florida. Presentation, August 1977.

Lammers, C.J. "Power and Participation in Decision-Making in Formal Organizations." *American Journal of Sociology* 73 (July 1967): 201–16.

Lawler, Edward E. and Hall, Douglas T. "The Relationships of Job Characteristics to Job Involvement, Satisfaction and Intrinsic Motivation." *Journal of Applied Psychology* 54 (August 1970): 305–12.

Lawler, Edward E. "Workers Can Set Their Own Wages-Responsibility." *Psychology Today* 10 (February 1977).

Lesieur, F.G. and Puckett, E.S. "The Scanlon Plan Has Proven Itself." *Harvard Business Review* 47 (October 1969): 109–18.

Levinson, Charles. *Industry's Democratic Revolution.* London: Allen and Unwin, 1974.

Likert, Rensis. *New Patterns of Management.* New York: McGraw Hill, 1961.

Lilienthal, David E. Carnegie Institute of Technology, New York. Presentation, April 1960.

Link, Ruth. "Shop-floor to Top-floor." *Sweden Now* 10 (1976): 18–48.

Lit, Theodore. "Expansion of Co-determination in West German Industry.' *Monthly Labor Review* 76 (April 1953): 393–95.

Loughran, Gerard. "Labor in Management? Both Hesitant." *The Atlanta Constitution* (August 22, 1977): 7D.

Lowin, Aaron. "Participative Decision Making: A Model, Literature Critique and Prescriptions for Research." *Organizational Behavior and Human Performance* 3 (February 1968): 68–106.

Lyon-caen, Gerard. "Beitrag zu den Möglichkeiten der Vertretung der Interessen der Arbeit nehmer in der Europaeischen Aktiengesellschaft." *Kollektive Studien, Reihe Wettbewerb-Rechtsangleichung*, 10, Brussels: 1970.

Maire, Edmond. "France." In *Industry's Democratic Revolution*, edited by Charles Levinson, pp. 324–31. London: Allen and Unwin, 1974.

Martin, Andrew. "From joint consultation to joint decision-making: The redistribution of workplace power in Sweden." In *Current Sweden*, pp. 1–11. New York: Swedish Institute, Swedish Consulate General, June 1976.

McIsaac, George S. "What's Coming in Labor Relations?" *Harvard Business Review* 55 (September–October 1977): 22–190.

Meyers, Frederic. "Workers' Control of Industry in Europe." *The Southwestern Social Science Quarterly* 39 (June 1958): 100–11.

Miles, Raymond E. "Human Relations or Human Resources?" In *Organizational Psychology*, edited by David A. Kolb, p. xx. Englewood Cliffs, N.J.: Prentice-Hall, 1971.

Miles, Raymond E. and J.B. Ritchie. "Participative Management: Quality vs. Quantity." *California Management Review* 13 (Summer 1971): 48–9.

"Mitbestimmung: Gut für die Koalition." *Der Spiegel* No. 50 (1975): 25–6.

Morgenthaler, Eric. "U.K. Report as Expected, Asks Big Firms to Put Labor on the Board." *The Wall Street Journal* 189 (January 27, 1977): 7.

Morse, N. and Reimer, E. "The Experimental Change of a Major Organizational Variable." *Journal of Abnormal and Social Psychology* 52 (1956): 120–29.

McElroy, Frank and Moros, Alexander. "Joint Production Committees, January 1948." *Monthly Labor Review* 67 (August 1948): 123–26.

McInnes, Neil. "Boardroom Revolution? In Great Britain, the Rights of Investors are in Jeopardy." *Barrons* 57 (February 14, 1977): 7.

_____. "Renault vs. Peugeot." *Barrons* 57 (May 30, 1977): 11–27.

_____. "People's Capitalism." *Barrons* 56 (July 12, 1976): 9.

McPherson, William. "Co-determination: Germany's Move Toward a New Economy." *Industrial and Labor Relations Review* 5 (October 1951): 20–32.

National Labor Relations Act: *Pennsylvania Greyhound Lines*, 303 U.S. 261, 1938.

The New Encyclopaedia Britannica. Chicago: Helen Hemingway Benton, 1974, Vol. 3, pp. 531–32.

Niedenhoff, Horst-Udo. *Mitbestimmung im Betrieb und Unternehmen.* Köln: Deutscher Instituts-Verlag GmbH, 1973.

Northrup, Bowen. "Battling Boredom." *The Wall Street Journal* (March 1, 1977): 1–36.

"Notice of 1976 Annual Meeting and Proxy Statement." New York: American Telephone and Telegraph Co., 1976.

Oates, David. "Argentinian Firm Introduces Self-Management," *International Management* 29 (November 1974): 55–8.

Obradovic, Josip. "Participation and Work Attitudes in Yugoslavia." *Industrial Relations* 9 (February 1970): 161–69.

"1976 Annual Meeting of Share Owners." New York: American Telephone and Telegraph Company, 1976.

Orr, David. "From the Boardroom." *Harvard Business Review* 55 (January–February 1977): 37–43.

"Participative Management at Work." *Harvard Business Review* 55 (January–February 1977): 117–26. Interview with Mr. John F. Donnelly.

Pasara, Luis and Jorge Santistevan. "Industrial Communities and Trade Unions in Peru: A Preliminary Analysis." *International Labour Review* 108 (August–September 1973): 127–42.

Patchen, M. "Labor-Management Consultation at TVA: Its Impact on Employees." *Administrative Science Quarterly* 10 (1965): 149–74.

Pearson, Donald W. "The Communidad Industrial: Peru's Experiment in Worker Management." *Inter-American Economic Affairs* 27 (Summer 1973): 17–31.

Prasad, S. Benjamin. "The Growth of Co-determination." *Business Horizons* 20 (April 1977): 23–9.

Prospero. "Inside Europe." *The Director* 25 (February 1973): 172.

_____. "Why BSC's Worker-Director Plan Flopped." *The Director* 24 (February 1972): 177.

Raskin, A.H. "The Heresy of Worker Participation." *Psychology Today* 10 (February 1977): 111.

Robinson, Richard D. "The Peruvian Experiment." Unpublished paper, The Sloan School of Management, Massachusetts Institute of Technology, April 1976.

Roeber, Joe. *Social Change at Work: The ICI Weekly Staff Agreement.* London: Gerald Duckworth, 1975.

Ruh, R. and White, J. "Effects of Personnel Values on the Relationship Between Participation and Job Attitudes." *Administrative Science Quarterly* 18 (December 1973): 506–14.

Ruh, R. et al. "Management Attitudes and the Scanlon Plan." *Industrial Relations* 12 (October 1973): 282–88.

Rukavina, Milan. "Yugoslavia." In *Industry's Democratic Revolution*, edited by Charles Levinson, pp. 153–85. London: Allen and Unwin, 1974.

Schleger, Hanns Martin. *Stellungnahme des Arbeitskreises Mitbestimmung zum Mitbestimmungsgesetz*. Köln: Bundesvereinigung der Deutschen Arbeitgeberverbände, 1976.

Schregle, Johannes. "Forms of Participation in Management." *Industrial Relations* 9 (February 1970): 117–23.

Serger, C.B. "Employee Representation and Personnel Work in a Large Scale Organization with Many Plants." *Proceedings of the Academy of Political Science* 9 (January 1922).

Shaw, Charles. "Management-Labor Committees." *Industrial and Labor Relations Review* 3 (January 1950): 229–41.

Smith, Kenneth S. "Sweden's Strange New Conservatism." *U.S. News and World Report* (February 20, 1978): 53–4.

Steinmetz, Dr. Jurgen. General-Council, August Thyssen Hütten Aktiengesellschaft, Duisburg-Hambon, West Germany. Letter, August 25, 1975.

Steins, Worker-director on the board of management of Hoesch AG, West Germany. Interview, August 1975.

Stolz, Walter. "How the Workers Participate in German Industry." *The Director* 27 (September 1974): 398.

"Stonewalling Plant Democracy." *Business Week* (March 28, 1977): 78–82.

Straaten, H.C. van, et al. *Benoeming van Commissarissen bij de grote NV en BV*. Den Haag, The Netherlands: Verbond van Nederlandse Ondernemingen, May 1972.

Sturmthal, Adolf F. "Unions and Industrial Democracy." *The Annals* 431 (May 1977): 12–21.

Thimm, Alfred L. "Recent Trends in German Co-determination Legislation and the Future of Capitalism in Europe." In *Administrative and Engineering Systems Monograph*, aes-7701, pp. 1–35. Schenectady, New York: Union College and University, January 1977.

_____. "Decision Making at Volkswagen 1972–1975." *Columbia Journal of World Business* 11 (Spring 1976): 94–103.

Thompson, James D. *Organization in Action*. New York: McGraw Hill, 1967.

Thorsrud, E. and Emery, F. "Industrial Democracy in Norway." *Industrial Relations* 9 (February 1970): 187–96.

Tittel, Roland. *Mitbestimmung: Forderungen und Tatsachen*. Köln: Deutsches Industrie-Institut, 1977.

U.S. Department of Labor. "Establishment of Industrial Councils in the Netherlands." *Monthly Labor Review* 36 (February 1933): 309–14.

_____. "Employee Representation in History." *Monthly Labor Review* 20 (April 1925): 759–62.

_____. "International Congress on Social Policy at Prague." *Monthly Labor Review* 19 (December 1924): 1385–87.

_____. "Operation of Works Committees in Czechoslovakia." *Monthly Labor Review* 19 (July 1924): 44–47.

_____. "Report on Joint Industrial Councils in England." *Monthly Labor Review* 17 (November 1923): 1017–19.

_____. "Yugoslav Law for the Protection of Workers." *Monthly Labor Review* 17 (September 1923): 159–66.

_____. "Operation of German Works Councils." *Monthly Labor Review* 16 (March 1923): 7–10.

_____. "Workmen's Committees in Czechoslovakia." *Monthly Labor Review* 13 (November 1921): 1147–48.

_____. "Collective Wage Agreements in Italy." *Monthly Labor Review* 13 (July 1921): 160–61.

_____. "Superior Labor Council of France." *Monthly Labor Review* 12 (June 1921): 1250–51.

_____. "Recent Developments in German Works Council System." *Monthly Labor Review* 12 (June 1921): 1251–53.

_____. "Labor Unrest in Germany." *Monthly Labor Review* 12 (April 1921): 871–85.

_____. "Austrian Law Establishing Chambers of Labor." *Monthly Labor Review* 10 (June 1920): 1495–97.

_____. "German Works Council Law." *Monthly Labor Review* 10 (May 1920): 256–65.

_____. "Joint Industrial Councils in Great Britain." *Monthly Labor Review* 9 (November 1919): 1538–39.

_____. "Austrian Law Establishing Works Councils." *Monthly Labor Review* 9 (September 1919): 741–42.

_____. "Final Report on Joint Industrial Councils, Great Britain." *Monthly Labor Review* 7 (December 1918): 1513–16.

U.S. Department of Labor. "Constitution and Functions of a Joint Industrial Council." *Monthly Labor Review* 7 (August 1918): 296–99.

_____. "British Government's Attitude on Joint Standing Industrial Councils." *Monthly Labor Review* 6 (March 1918): 573.

_____. "Proposed Joint Standing Industrial Councils in Great Britain." *Monthly Labor Review* 5 (September 1917): 532–44.

_____. "Colorado Fuel and Iron Company Industrial Representation Plan." *Monthly Labor Review* 1 (December 1915): 12–22.

Van Haren, Ivo A. Supervisory Board, Akzo Nederland B.V., Velp, The Netherlands. Interview, August 1975.

Van Haren, Ivo A.C. *Naar een nieuwe ondernemingsstructuur.* Assen, The Netherlands: Van Gorcum, N.V., 1967.

Van Heijningen, R. Hoorens and Vermeulen, Mr. Dutch Employers Federation, Verbond van Nederlandse Ondernemingen VNO, The Hague, The Netherlands. Interview, August 1975.

Vikland, Birger. "Education for Industrial Democracy." *Working Life in Sweden*, edited by Swedish Information Service, pp. 1–4. New York: Swedish Consulate General, May 1977.

Vogl, Frank. *German Business After the Economic Miracle.* New York: Halsted Press, 1973.

Ways, Max. "The American Kind of Worker Participation." *Fortune* 94 (October 1976): 168–82.

Weigart, Oscar. "Co-determination in Western Germany." *Monthly Labor Review* 73 (December 1951): 649–56.

"When Workers Help Call the Tune in Management." *U.S. News and World Report* 80 (May 10, 1976): 83–5.

Whitney, Anice. "Employees' Representation." *Monthly Labor Review* 9 (November 1919): 1527–29.

"Who Manages Whom." *The Economist* 240 (August 21, 1971): 22–5.

Whyte, William Foote and Giorgio Alberti. "The Industrial Community in Peru." *The Annals* 431 (May 1977): 103–12.

Wiardi, Beckman Stichting. *Op weg naar Arbeiderszelfbestuur.* Deventer, The Netherlands: Kluwer, 1974.

Windmuller, John P. "Preface." *The Annals* 431 (May 1977): 7–8.

Woodcock, Leonard. "U.S.A." In *Industry's Democratic Revolution*, edited by Charles Levinson, pp. 199–218. London: Allen and Unwin, 1974.

"Work Committees in France." *International Labour Review* 51 (June 1945): 770–75.

"Work Committees in France." *International Labour Review* 95 (April 1967): 356–58.

"Workers Help Management." *Time* 39 (June 15, 1942): 81–2.

"Workers on the Board." *The Economist* 246 (March 24, 1973): 67.

"Workers on the Board." *Forbes* 11 (June 1976): 66–7.

"Workers on the Board." *Time* 105 (May 19, 1975): 57.

"Works Committees in Denmark." *International Labour Review* 57 (April 1948): 365–76.

Zagoria, Sam. "Policy Implications and Future Agenda." In *The Worker and the Job*, edited by American Assembly, pp. 177–201. Englewood Cliffs, N.J.: Prentice-Hall, 1974.

Zalusky, John L. Economist, Research Department AFL-CIO. Letter, January 29, 1976.

INDEX

Adam Opel A. G., 37, 83
AFL-CIO, 82; and co-determination, 103
Akzo-Nederland B. V., 45, 59, 83, 87, 89, 100
AKZO N. V., 100
Allamanna Svenska Elektriska AB, 48
Allianz-Leben, 82
American Multigraph Company, 13
Angestellte: definition, 4
Atlantic Refining Company, 13
Atwood Vacuum Machine Company, 16
August Thyssen-Hütte, A. G., 59
Avon Cosmetics GmbH, 37

BASF, 83
Basic Organization of Associated Labor, 73
Bayer, 83
Bethlehem Steel Corporation, 82
Biedenkopf Commission, 2, 84
board of directors: comparison with super-
    visory and management boards, 5–6;
    description of tasks, 4–6
board of management: definition, 5
British North German Iron and Steel Control
    Board, 21
British Reconstruction Committee, 18 (see
    also Whitley Committee)
British Steel Corporation, 52
Bullock Proposal, 51, 53–4; European
    Company Statute vs., 57–9; German
    co-determination vs., 54

Chicago Federation of Labor and Industrial
    Union Council, 82
Chrysler, 82, 104, 105
co-determination: in Austria, 61–2; in
    Belgium, 45; Bullock Proposal and
    European Company Statute vs., 57;
    controversial topic, 8; definition, 4; in
    Denmark, 47; in the European Eco-
    nomic Community, 54–60 (see also
    European Company Statute); in the
    Federal Republic of Germany, 28–39;
    in France, 60–1 (see also Sudreau
    proposal); in Ireland, 62; in Italy, 62;
    and loss of control, 97–100; in Luxem-
    bourg, 45–6; means to reduce union
    power, 82–3; multinationals and, 95–

100; in the Netherlands, 41–5; in
    Norway, 46–7; stalemates and
    compromises, 83–5; in Sweden, 47–8;
    union power and, 80–2; in the United
    Kingdom, 51–4 (see also Bullock pro-
    posal); in the United States, 100–108;
    West German Act of 1976, 28, 36–9;
    West German Law of 1951, 22, 28–31;
    West German Law of 1956, 28, 31;
    white-collar workers and, 88–9; work-
    ers and, 85–8
collective bargaining: co-determination and,
    90–2
Colorado Fuel and Iron Company, 12 (see
    also Rockefeller plan)
competency of workers' representatives, 89–
    90
Continental Roll and Steel Foundry, 14
control: and co-determination, 97–100
councils: joint district, 3; joint industrial, 3,
    18; joint production, 3, 14; works, 3;
    workshop, 3

Deutsche Goodyear GmbH, 37
Deutsche Texaco, A. G., 37
Douglas Aircraft Corporation, 14

Eastman Kodak, 95, 96 (see also Kodak
    A. G.)
Elgin Watch Company, 14
employees: distinction between type of, 4
employee participation: definition, 4; in the
    Federal Republic of Germany, 22; (see
    also co-determination, worker partici-
    pation)
Enka-Glanzstoff, 59, 100 (see also Akzo)
Esso A. G., 37 (see also Exxon)
ESTEL N. V., 31, 56
European Company Statute, 55–60; future of,
    59–60; U. K., West Germany vs.,
    54–9; unions and, 60
executives: U. S. and co-determination, 105–
    07
Exxon, 95 (see also Esso A. G.)

Filene Department Store, 11

Ford Motor Corporation, 82, 95, 105 (*see also* Ford Werke A. G.)
Ford Werke A. G., 37 (*see also* Ford Motor Corporation)
Foreign direct investments: and co-determination, 37, 96

General Electric Company, 15
General Foods, 95
General Motors, 82, 95, 105, 107
Goodyear, 95

Harwood Manufacturing Company, 15
Hoesch, A. G., 31–4, 56, 59, 83, 91

IBM, 95, 96 (*see also* Deutschland GmbH)
IBM Deutschland GmbH, 37 (*see also* IBM)
I. G. Metall, 81
Imperial Chemical Industries, 4, 52–3, 59, 83, 87, 92
Independent Pneumatic Tool Company, 14
industrial communities, 75–7
industrial councils or committees: in Belgium, 19, 21, 23; in the Netherlands, 20; in the United Kingdom, 18, 20–1 (*see also* Whitley Committee)
interest groups: connected with the organization, 1
International Federation of Chemicals Workers' Unions, 102
International Harvester, 95
International Petroleum Company, 75
ITT, 95

joint production committee, 14
joint ventures: and co-determination, 98–9

Kodak A. G., 37 (*see also* Eastman Kodak)
Koninklijke Nederlandsche Hoogovens, 31, 56

Leitch, John: employee representation plan, 12, 13
Leitende Angestellte: definition, 4

management board: definition, 4 (*see also* board of management)
Mannesmannrohren-Werke, 84
Mannesmann Steel Pipe Company, 81
Minnesota Mining and Manufacturing, 95
Mitbestimmung, 4 (*see also* co-determination in the Federal Republic of Germany)

Mobil Oil A. G., 83 (*see also* Mobil Oil Company)
Mobil Oil Company, 95 (*see also* Mobil Oil A. G.)
multinationals: and co-determination, 96–100

Nerst Lamp Company, 12

Occidental Life, 82
Opel (*see* Adam Opel A. G.)
ownership: and co-determination, 97–100

Packard Piano Company, 12
Parker Pen Company, 16
participative decision making: definition, 3–4
Pfaudler Company, 16
Philips N. V., 42, 59, 83, 87, 89
Procter and Gamble Company, 95
productivity: and participation, 14–17

research: design, methodology and strategy, 6–9
Rockefeller plan, 19 (*see also* Colorado Fuel and Iron Company)

satisfaction: and participation, 15–17
Scanlon, Joseph: plan, 13–14, 16–17
self-management system, 73–5
shop committee: condemned, 13; first known, 12; U. S. government and, 12
Siemens A. G., 59
stakeholders: primary and secondary, 5
Standard Oil of New Jersey, 75
Steel Trustee Association, 21
Sudreau proposal, 61
supervisory board: definition, 4–5

Tennessee Valley Authority, 15
Texaco, 95

Unilever, 59, 82, 89
unions: co-determination and the U. S., 102–105
Union Labor Life Insurance Company, 82
United Automobile Workers Union, 82, 104
United States Steel, 82

Verbond van Nederlandse Ondernemingen, 83
Volksfürsorge-Lebensversicherung, 82
Volkswagen, 81

WCFL, 82

Western Union Telegraph Company, 13
Westinghouse Electric Company, 14
Whitley Committee, 18, 20 (*see also* industrial
    councils)
worker participation: in Austria, 61–62; in the
    European Economic Community, 56–
    7; in the Federal Republic of Germany,
    28–39; in France, 24, 60–1; in Italy,
    62; in the Netherlands, 24; in Norway,
    24; in Peru, 75–6; in Sweden, 24; in
    the United Kingdom, 51–4 (*see also*
    Bullock Proposal); in Yugoslavia, 72–
    5 (*see also* co-determination, industrial
    councils, participative decision making,

participative management, works
    councils)
workers: U. S.- and co-determination, 108
Works Constitution Act of 1952, 31, 34
works council, 2; in Austria, 19, 21, 61–2; in
    Belgium, 19, 23, 45; in Czecho-
    slovakia, 19, in Denmark, 22; in the
    European Economic Community, 56;
    in France, 21, 24; in the Federal
    Republic of Germany, 19, 34–6; in
    Italy, 22, 62; in Ireland, 62; in the
    Netherlands, 41–2; in Yugoslavia,
    73–5

ABOUT THE AUTHOR

ROBERT J. KÜHNE is Assistant Professor of Business Administration and the Associate Director of the Master in International Business Studies (MIBS) program at The University of South Carolina, Columbia, South Carolina. He is an active international business consultant as well.

Dr. Kühne has published widely in the area of international management. His articles have appeared in the *Columbia Journal of World Business* and *Business Horizons*. Professor Kühne is Associate Editor of the *Journal of Business Research*. He appeared in many U.S. and foreign television interviews on a wide variety of international business topics.

Dr. Kühne, a resident of The Netherlands, holds a certificate of Institut International Valcreuse, Lausanne, Switzerland; a degree from Nijenrode, The Netherlands Institut of Business, Breukelen, The Netherlands; and an M.B.A. and Ph.D. from The University of Georgia, Athens, Georgia.